5.8m (66 by 19ft) video screens show the races in progress, as well as the state of the betting, racing forms and other relevant data. The total amount bet every season is the highest of any racecourse in the world, with much of the profits donated to charity. *See also Sport, p.112.*

for their rattan and rosewood furniture shops. A few remain, and have been joined by slick interior design furniture stores, luxury car showrooms and restaurants. It is worth taking a look also at two traditional temples that stand in stark contrast to their modern surroundings. Tiny, dark **Hung Shing Temple** ③ on Queen's Road East (by Tai Wing Street) was named after a Tang-dynasty official who was renowned for his ability to make valuable predictions for traders.

The impressive **Pak Tai Temple** ④ at the top of Stone Nullah Lane is a triple-halled building noted for its 400-year-old, 3m (10ft) statue of the deity Pak Tai, who assures harmony on earth. There are usually elderly locals pottering around in the dark recesses of the temple, lighting incense sticks or laying out offerings.

Causeway Bay Shopping

Nowhere is the relationship between the Hong Kong dollar and the shopping bag more visible than in the retail forest that is Causeway Bay. Known locally as 'Little Japan', it is packed with designer boutiques, cosmetics shops and department stores, and is nothing short of a shopper's heaven, albeit a polluted one. If you cannot find it here, it probably does not exist.

Japanese department store **Sogo** on Hennessy

Leafy Bowen Road is almost car-free and popular with joggers and walkers. It makes for a lush urban walk with panoramic views. Take bus 15 and get off at the Adventist Hospital and walk west. Look out for the phallic-shaped Lover's Rock, a place of pilgrimage for many hoping for babies or husbands.

Road is a landmark, and every kind of shop can be found in mega-malls like Times Square, while nearby Muji, Uniqlo and more Japanese brands and some interesting local designers can be found around **Great George Street** in mini-malls such as **Island Beverley** and the **Fashion Walk**. For a rest, just to the west there is the tranquil green space of **Victoria Park**.
SEE ALSO PARKS AND GARDENS, P.85; SHOPPING, P.99, 100

Happy Valley

Continue eastwards on a Happy Valley-bound tram for another 15 minutes or so and you will arrive at **Happy Valley Racecourse** ⑤. A visit to the Wednesday-night races during the September to June racing season is a must, but during the day it is worth calling in at the **Hong Kong Racing Museum**, at the Happy Valley Stand inside the racecourse, which tells the story of horse racing in the colony with plenty of colourful background on the equestrian obsession that, twice a week, holds much of Hong Kong to ransom.
SEE ALSO MUSEUMS AND GALLERIES, P.66; SPORT, P.112

11

The Southside

Despite being home to over a quarter of a million people – the southside of Hong Kong remains a green and pleasant contrast to the unfeasibly-crowded urbanised strip along the north shore. The rides and dolphins at Ocean Park are a major draw, while elsewhere there are some fine beaches for swimming, surfing or just sunbathing; the engaging waterfront town of Stanley with its relaxed streetlife, market and pleasant seaside villages like Shek O are easy to reach for half or full day outings. The MTR's South Island Line will reach as far southeast as Ocean Park when it opens in 2015.

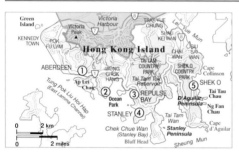

On your way to Stanley, look out for a large blue apartment building called The Repulse Bay, with a big square hole in the middle. Some say the hole is a passageway for the heavenly dragon to come down from the mountains; others that it was put there to generate good *feng shui*; others that it was simply the architect's attempt at being funky.

Aberdeen ①

The harbour town of Aberdeen has a character unlike any other part of Hong Kong, and is immediately recognisable for its flotilla of bobbing junks and sampans. This waterside community resides in one of the island's few natural typhoon shelters, and consists of two main groups: the *Tanka* (literally, 'the egg people', because they used to pay taxes with eggs rather than cash) and the *Hoklo*.

Tourists often get a ringside view of life on the harbour during the boat shuttle journey to one of the world's largest floating restaurants, the unmissable **Jumbo Kingdom**. These famous boats include shops, a museum and even a Chinese culinary academy. Aberdeen's commercial attractions do not only relate to eating, either, for on the offshore island of Ap Lei Chau is the hugely popular **Horizon Plaza** discount warehouse and factory store.

SEE ALSO RESTAURANTS, P.91; SHOPPING, P.103

Left: Stanley Beach.

TIN HAU TEMPLE

A trip to Aberdeen is not complete without a visit to the island's Tin Hau Temple on Aberdeen Main Road, and particularly during the **Tin Hau Festival** in April or May.

Tin Hau is the goddess of the sea and a traditionally important figure in the fishing community, and there are temples honouring her all over Hong Kong. At festival time thousands of boats converge on Aberdeen's shores, and the temple is decorated with paper shrines and lanterns. Highly charged and photogenic lion dances are performed outside.

Ocean Park ②

Ocean Park celebrated its 35th anniversary in 2012, making it relatively ancient by Hong Kong standards.

Adjacent to Murray House is Blake Pier, featuring a 1909 pavilion salvaged from Blake Pier in Central. The **Old Stanley Police Station** is a declared monument and now home to a supermarket. The quirky **Correctional Services Museum** relates the history of Hong Kong's prisons. Near the prison is **Stanley Military Cemetery**, with tombstones dating to early colonial times.

Around the coast from Stanley, in the southeast corner of the island, **Shek O** is one of its most laid-back villages. It is best known for adjacent **Big Wave Bay**, the haunt of Hong Kong surfers.
SEE ALSO MUSEUMS AND GALLERIES, P.65

But thanks to a combination of its seaside setting on a headland overlooking the South China Sea and continual investment, the theme park remains perennially popular with locals and a must-see for visiting families. A cable-car ride with spectacular views is a highlight, and the 80-hectare (200-acre) park houses rides, an aquarium with 2,000 sea creatures and two giant pandas. A new funicular rail system transports visitors from the lowland to the headland areas.
SEE ALSO CHILDREN, P.32

Repulse Bay ③

Primarily an upmarket residential area, sun-drenched Repulse Bay (named after the British battleship HMS *Repulse*), has a relaxed, resort-like atmosphere. The wide, wave-lapped beach is great for sandy strolls in the early morning, when the sun is up and the sunbathers are starting to come out in force, or at sunset when all is at peace. This crescent-shaped stretch of sand is one of the most beautiful beaches in Hong Kong, and picturesque gardens lead down to it. The nearby colonial-style Repulse Bay development houses designer shops and award-winning restaurants.

Stanley ④ and Shek O ⑤

With its relaxed seaside ambience and sprawling cluster of market stalls, Stanley Market is a great place to stock up on bargains. Its boardwalk promenade, and open-fronted restaurants make this an easy place to potter for a relaxed day out. Stanley is now home to **Murray House**, a former British Army barracks built in 1848, dismantled, and moved stone by stone from the site now filled by the Bank of China tower in Central.

Beyond Ocean Park to the east is a region of rocky coasts and white sand that contains 11 of Hong Kong's 40 beaches that are considered suitable for swimming. A few locations, such as **Rocky Bay** on the road to **Shek O**, have virtually no public facilities but offer unparalleled views and uncrowded stretches of sand and sea. Others, like **Repulse Bay**, attract bus loads of tourists and, at weekends, offer about as much peace and quiet as a carnival.

Deep Water Bay ⑤, the first beach east of Ocean Park, has some beautiful mansions, and is reputed to enjoy some of the best *feng shui* in Hong Kong. It also has a nine-hole golf course managed by the Hong Kong Golf Club (open weekdays to the public). Further along the road towards Stanley is the exclusive Hong Kong Country Club. The long stretch of beach here offers a quiet place to soak up the sun or go for a swim.
See also Sport, p.112, 113.

Kowloon

Though not short of the malls and hotels Hong Kong is known for, sprawling Kowloon is in many ways the Chinese alter ego of bold, modern Central. Its waterfront has some of Hong Kong's biggest recent constructions, in the mall-space of Harbour City or the giant K-11 tower, iSquare and One Peking Road, while along the great snake of Nathan Road, the landmark gaudy array of discount electronics stores have been joined by acres of gold jewellery shops. Leave commercial Kowloon behind, however, and you will find in its streets and markets genuine pockets of Chinese-ness that will transport you far from the glamour of 21st-century Hong Kong.

The Waterfront

The **Star Ferry Pier** ①, with its adjacent **Railway Clock Tower**, the sweeping curve of the **Hong Kong Cultural Centre** and the igloo-like **Hong Kong Space Museum** are the Tsim Sha Tsui waterfront's most prominent landmarks.

Dating from 1915, the railway tower is the last vestige of the historic **Kowloon-Canton Railway Station**, once the final stop in a system that ran all the way to Europe. The waterfront promenade offers unparalleled views of the harbour and Hong Kong Island, and is now also known for its **Avenue of Stars** along Salisbury Road, a star-studded path honouring

Above: the high-rise flats on the coast of Kowloon.

the city's film glitterati.

To the west, is Hong Kong's tallest building **ICC** and the site of the terminus for the new Hong Kong Guang-zhou rail terminus – scheduled to open in 2015 – to connect the SAR to China's national high-speed

rail network,

SEE ALSO FILM, P.45; MUSEUMS AND GALLERIES, P.67; MUSIC, DANCE AND THEATRE, P.74; TEMPLES AND HISTORIC SITES, P.115; TRANSPORT, P.124

Tsim Sha Tsui

TST, as this southern tip of Kowloon is known, is the commercial honeypot that attracts the tourist bees. The heart of Tsim Sha Tsui is known as the 'Golden Mile', its central axis, which actually rolls on for far more than a mile (1.6km) of **Nathan Road** ②.

Lacking the steep mountainsides that hem in the north shore of Hong Kong Island, Kowloon sprawls in every sense of the word. But with Nathan Road as its spine, and peppered with MTR stations, it is very easy to navigate.

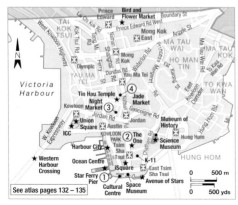

See atlas pages 132 – 135

Left: the Kowloon Bird Market.

renewal is translated into new skyscrapers, hotels and even more shops, bars and restaurants, especially around **K-11** on Hart Avenue.
SEE ALSO MUSEUMS AND GALLERIES, P.66, 67

Yau Ma Tei and Mong Kok

Street markets and old buildings have escaped demolition in these areas further north along Nathan Road, making them great places to explore. The **Flower**, **Goldfish** and **Bird** markets, **Temple Street Night Market** ③ and famous **Jade Market** ④ are all here. These areas can provide fascinating vignettes of local life, and are home to a clutch of Hong Kong's most interesting temples, such as the **Tin Hau Temple** in Yau Ma Tei.
SEE ALSO SHOPPING, P.101, 102; TEMPLES AND HISTORIC SITES, P.115

ALONG NATHAN ROAD

Named for the former Governor Sir Matthew Nathan, whose central urban planning and reconstruction policy led to the development of several major thoroughfares on the Kowloon peninsula, today Nathan Road is a mecca for visitors from China and has newer, more stylish shopping options, such as **The One** and **iSquare** malls. Host to the Hong Kong image of gaudy neon signs and end-

less gold jewellery and electronics shops, it is not always an attractive place, but few can deny the electricity of life here, especially at night.
SEE ALSO SHOPPING, P.99, 100

SHOPPING AND DINING

The main shopping and entertainment area of Tsim Sha Tsui extends either side of the MTR station: around **Peking**, **Hankow** and **Haiphong** roads on the western side, and **Carnarvon** and **Kimberley** roads to the east. There are excellent shopping and dining pockets here, with hundreds of restaurants. The Kowloon renaissance is particularly evident along Canton Road, TST and Langham Place in Mongkok.

On the east of Nathan Road towards the **Hong Kong Museum of History** and **Hong Kong Science Museum**, near the new East TST MTR station, urban

Kowloon's Changing Face

Until Kai Tak Airport closed in the late 1990s, regulations restricted Kowloon's buildings to a modest height. Now, they shoot skywards as never before. The most obvious is West Kowloon above Kowloon MTR station. The Union Square development includes Elements shopping mall and the 484m (1,588ft) International Commerce Centre (ICC) the city's tallest building. Land in front of the ICC has been earmarked for an extensive 'cultural district'. Design disputes have stalled the project inadvertently providing Hong Kongers with a fabulous harbourside space for occasional festivals and concerts. Among the buildings that have already pierced the Kowloon sky are The Masterpiece on Hanoi Road, One Peking on Peking Road, and Langham Place, a multi-use mall, hotel and office complex *(see p.59)*.

Left: neon signs, Nathan Road.

15

New Kowloon

Traditionally, Kowloon ended at Boundary Street – so-called because it marks the boundary between the Colony of Hong Kong and the territory leased from China in 1898 along with what is now called the New Territories. Long integrated into Kowloon's urban landscape, New Kowloon includes the districts of Sham Shui Po, Kowloon Tong, Wong Tai Sin, Kowloon City and Kwun Tong. The urban forest that characterises these areas is juxtaposed with historic architecture, temples and archaeological ruins and – if you know where to look, among the densely populated housing estates and shopping malls – it is possible to find some real Hong Kong gems.

Sham Shui Po

To the northwest of Mong Kok, the old districts of Sham Shui Po and **Cheung Sha Wan** are easily accessed by MTR. Sham Shui Po is the place to head (as locals do) for computers and related merchandise, with a huge assortment of arcades and stalls around the junction of

---

The **Chi Lin Nunnery** ① (close to Diamond Hill MTR) is the largest Buddhist nunnery in Southeast Asia, and a living museum of the Tang dynasty (618–907). The nunnery comprises a number of Buddhist halls serving various functions, and lotus ponds flank the main entrance. Across the road Nian Lin Garden (daily 7am–9pm; free) is a tranquil garden also following Tang aesthetics with a vegetarian snack bar and restaurant. *See also Temples and Historic Sites, p.115.*

Right: Wong Tai Sin Temple.

Yen Chow and Fuk Wa streets. All along **Apliu Street** there is an open-air market selling cheap electrical goods, and many of the latest gizmos, from iPods to DVD players, are *sui foh*: imported directly from Japan, and so available at lower prices. Be prepared, though, because the service style is often hectic and high-pressure, and rip-offs do occur. Check items carefully before parting with your cash.

Wong Tai Sin

Probably the liveliest and most colourful place of worship in Hong Kong, and one of the most rewarding for outsiders to visit, is **Wong Tai Sin Temple** ②, sitting opposite the MTR station of the same name, and easily recognisable by its bright-yellow roof tiling. Backed by

the formidable Lion Rock and facing the sea, this shrine to the Taoist god of healing has *feng shui* in spades. The rear of the main altar is carved to show, both pictorially and in calligraphy, the story of this great god. There are two gardens surrounding the temple and a Confucian hall next door, and English-speaking

Kowloon City is known for cheap, rough-and-ready restaurants that serve dishes within minutes of ordering. If you don't mind high-decibel dining, or sharing a table with strangers, then the area has some inexpensive and highly rated Thai restaurants, plus a handful of hole-in-the-wall diners specialising in regional Chinese cuisine.

fortune-tellers are on hand to predict your future.

SEE ALSO TEMPLES AND HISTORIC SITES, P.116

Kowloon City

Within New Kowloon, just south of Wong Tai Sin, this area's name commemorates the once-famous **Kowloon Walled City** ③, a place with a unique history within Hong Kong. A fortress was built here by the Chinese government in the 19th century, governed by a Manchu magistrate; hence it was excluded from the treaty that granted Britain the New Territories on a 99-year lease in 1898. The Walled City was thus outside the laws of the British colony, from criminal laws to building regulations, and by the 1950s the area had become a notorious slum, a centre of criminality with some of Hong Kong's worst housing.

In 1992, the Walled City was demolished and much of

its former site landscaped as an attractive city park. Kowloon City is easily explored on foot, starting at Lok Fu MTR station. As well as the park, other sites include the **Chinese Christian Cemetery**, with its graves stacked up like sardines on concrete terraces, and the tiny **Hau Wong Temple**.

Plans to redevelop the site of Kai Tak airport including a new cruise terminal, malls, a sports stadium, luxury housing and a monorail, are expected to revitalise Kowloon City.

KOWLOON WALLED CITY PARK

Laid out like a classic garden of southern China, the park seeks to preserve something of the heritage of Kowloon's fabled Walled City. Several remnants – the foundation of the former wall, large parts of

the Walled City's south and east gates, and a flagstone path next to the drainage ditch along the foot of the inner wall – have been preserved. Other attractions include a chess garden, the **Mountain View Pavilion**, from which Lion Rock (495m/1,625ft) can be seen looming in the distance, sculptures, pavilions and attractive pathways lined with trees and flower borders. Near the southern gate, an information centre houses a photographic exhibition detailing the history of the Walled City and the construction of the park, as well as many relics used or found within the Walled City.

The New Territories

Hong Kong's northern hinterland is well off the tourist trail, which seems surprising given its calm beaches, lofty mountains, forests and ancient walled villages. Acting as a buffer between Kowloon and the boundary with Mainland China, the towns and villages of the New Territories are an odd mix of the traditional and the very modern. This is home to half of Hong Kong's population, and spectacular country parks. Many visitors don't realise just how much countryside the Territory possesses. Exploring is easy, with access on the MTR, Light Rail and a network of buses that reach into most corners.

Left: Hakka woman wearing a traditional fringed hat and a rare smile.

Sha Tin Racecourse

Hong Kong's first and largest 'new town', **Sha Tin** is home to a handful of attractions, notably the **Hong Kong Heritage Museum** and the racecourse. Happy Valley tends to steal Sha Tin's thunder on the international stage, but to overlook this magnificent course is a great shame: it is a bigger course, it has racing all weekend rather than just one night a week, and it now hosts all local racing's blue-riband events, such as the Hong Kong Derby.

Sha Tin Racecourse ① can hold some 78,000 spectators, and has a massive Diamond Vision Video Screen (70.4m/230ft high) that is one of the largest in the world. Betting pools regularly reach into the hundreds of millions of dollars. In terms of sheer pageantry Chinese New Year

is possibly the best time to come here, but race days are never short of excitement – or crowds.
SEE ALSO MUSEUMS AND GALLERIES, P.65; SPORT, P.112

SHA TIN'S TEMPLES

The Sha Tin Valley has several places of worship, but first and foremost is the

Temple of 10,000 Buddhas ②, reached by climbing 431 steps flanked by gold-painted effigies of enlightened beings up the hillside above Sha Tin station. The temple's main altar room actually has 12,800 Buddha statues along its walls. A further 69 steps up the hill is the **Temple of Man Fat**, containing the preserved remains of the monk who created this temple-pagoda complex, Yuet Kai.

From the Temple of 10,000 Buddhas you can look across the valley at **Amah Rock**, said to resemble an *amah*, or nanny, with a

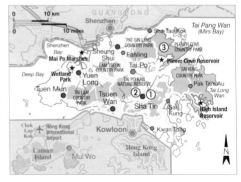

Left: Hoi Mei Wang Beach, an isolated retreat.

The Walled Villages of the New Territories trace their roots to the 10th century, when the 'five clans' moved here from further north, near Guangzhou, and built these fortified settlements to protect themselves from marauding outsiders, and each other. Later villages were occupied by the *Hakka*, North Chinese migrants settled here by government decree in the 17th–18th centuries, and who lived apart from the Cantonese. The way of life in the walled villages remains fairly traditional, so it is worth paying the small donation to enter. The price for taking a picture of a *Hakka* woman wearing a traditional fringed hat will vary depending on your bargaining skills, and do not expect a smile. *See also Temples and Historic Sites, p.116.*

baby on her back. A place of worship for Chinese women, it stands as a symbol of women's loyalty and fidelity.
SEE ALSO TEMPLES AND HISTORIC SITES, P.117

Plover Cove and Sai Kung Peninsula

The northeast corner of the New Territories is one of Hong Kong's least developed areas. Once home only to remote villages of farming and fishing communities, it also includes large stretches of remarkably wild countryside, coast and mountain, excellent for hiking and bird-watching. At **Plover Cove** ③ visitors can obtain information on walks and nature trails around the nearby **Plover Cove Reservoir**.

Just to the south, the **Sai Kung peninsula** is a designated recreational area and a popular destination for local walkers, picnickers, swimmers and sailors.

SAI KUNG COUNTRY PARK

The convoluted coastline of the New Territories includes some fine stretches of beach – nowhere more so than at **Tai Long Wan** on the eastern edge of Sai Kung, where powdery white sands meet some relatively decent surf. Kill two birds with one stone and get here (it takes about an hour's hike) along part of the **Mac Lehose Trail**, which starts in Sai Kung Country Park and stretches for 100km (60 miles) through mostly open country. Join the trail at **Pak Tam Au**.

Some of Hong Kong's most enjoyable outer islands sit in the inner Port Shelter, offshore from Sai Kung Village. Sampan owners will make a 1hr trip for around HK$150 to whichever island you wish, or charge around HK$400 to drop you at your destination and collect you later. Whichever you decide to do, bargain hard!

Sai Kung town itself is known for its string of seaside restaurants, which line the busy quayside. You can also take a sampan from here to some of Hong Kong's outlying islands *(see box, left)*.

Other Nature Reserves

Tolo Harbour north of Sai Kung, the Mirs Bay islands to the east and the **Hong Kong Wetland Park** in the Mai Po marshes in Deep Bay are all worth exploring. But one of the best places to escape urban Hong Kong is the Tai Po Kau Nature Reserve, a short taxi ride from Tai Po Market MTR station. Planting began here in 1926, and today the 450-hectare (1,110-acre) forest shelters a good proportion of Hong Kong's flora and fauna.
SEE ALSO CHILDREN, P.32

The Outer Islands

Hong Kong's outlying islands are a breath of fresh air in what can sometimes be a stifling city. But as well as being good for the constitution, a visit to laid-back Lantau, Cheung Chau, Lamma, tiny Peng Chau or – with a bit more exploration – some of the smallest and more remote islands can offer an insight into a way of life that is fast disappearing in Hong Kong. The islands are also home to some of the SAR's most beautiful temples and most vibrant festivals. Take at least half a day and if possible a bit longer to explore, adapt to the pace, and you will be rewarded with memories far removed from the hurly-burly of the city.

Above: Tai O fishing harbour, Lantau.

Each year Cheung Chau hosts its four-day **Bun Festival**, when giant bamboo towers covered with edible buns are erected in the courtyard of Pak Tai Temple. In the past, local boys climbed the towers to pluck their lucky buns, and the higher the bun, the more luck it would bring. These days, it is trained athletes who risk their necks.
See also Festivals, p.40.

Lantau

Majestic and ruggedly mountainous, Lantau is often referred to as Hong Kong's green lung. More than twice the size of Hong Kong Island, it has country parks, beaches and coastal villages that make it a popular retreat for day-trippers and weekenders. Lantau remains largely rural, but inevitably the peace and seclusion of much of the island, typified by the Buddhist monasteries dotted around the mountain slopes, is steadily being eroded. Hong Kong International Airport lies on its northwestern coast, while **Hong Kong Disneyland** ① now occupies a giant site on the island's eastern tip at Penny's Bay. Lantau's main sights can be covered in a day, but avoid

public holidays, when the ferries are packed.
SEE ALSO CHILDREN, P.32

TEMPLE IN THE CLOUDS

Lantau's main draw is its bronze 202-tonne Big Buddha, which peers down over the **Po Lin Monastery** ② complex. Po Lin is the largest of Hong Kong's Buddhist temples, a sprawling complex

of temples, gateways and gardens, and a major point of pilgrimage for Hong Kong's Buddhists. Founded in 1905 by three humble monks who wanted a quiet retreat away from the hustle and bustle of Hong Kong, it also has an excellent vegetarian restaurant for its visitors.
SEE ALSO TEMPLES AND HISTORIC SITES, P.117; WALKS AND VIEWS, P.129

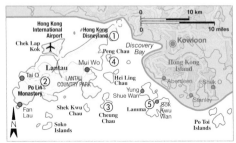

Left: the Big Buddha at Po Lin Monastery.

way to explore this island is by foot or bicycle. It is also an island of two halves. The small village of **Yung Shue Wan** is the main population centre. Despite a frequent ferry service to Central, the island remains slow-paced, and Yung Shue Wan's seaside vibe draws in both Chinese and foreigners seeking a greener way of life. A handful of shops, restaurants, pubs and cafés line the waterfront, and there's a family-friendly beach at Hung Sing Yeh, some 20 minutes from the ferry pier. **Sok Kwu Wan**, a 90-minute walk across the island, is only visited for its string of Chinese seafood restaurants.

SEE ALSO WALKS AND VIEWS, P.129

Cheung Chau ③

Dumbbell-shaped Cheung Chau, just south of Lantau, offers some good walks, fine beaches, a handful of temples dedicated to Tin Hau, goddess of the sea, and is known for throwing some of Hong Kong's most exuberant and colourful festivals, such as the **Bun Festival** *(see opposite)*.

Cheung Chau village has a lively waterfront atmosphere. The waterfront promenade, the **praya**, is one of Hong Kong's most pleasant alfresco dining spots, especially after sunset. Head off in any direction from the ferry terminal and you will find both modern and traditional shops and restaurants. The village, around the ferry dock, is a tangle of interesting alleyways best explored at leisure; if you get lost, simply steer yourself back downhill.

Cheung Chau also offers

excellent **windsurfing**, centred on **Tung Wan**.

SEE ALSO SPORT, P.113

Peng Chau ④

About a third of the size of Cheung Chau, and linked to it by an inter-island ferry service as well as to the main Hong Kong ferry piers, Peng Chau is so small that you can walk around the island in an hour. Past the excessive concrete of the sea wall, inland is the 200-year-old **Tin Hau Temple** and the **Kum Fa Temple**, dedicated to Lady Kum Fa, who is said to help fertility.

SEE ALSO TEMPLES AND HISTORIC SITES, P.115

Lamma ⑤

Characterised by grassy hills, picturesque bays and easy walks and bike trails, Lamma is instantly identifiable by the three chimneys of its power station and lone windmill. Free of motor vehicles, the only

For information on island ferries, *see Transport, p.124.* The three key islands are accessible in under 1hr (or as quickly as 25min on the faster ferries) from the Central Ferry Piers. Services are frequent and inexpensive. Alternatively, the Island Hopping Pass allows unlimited daytime travel to Cheung Chau, Lantau and Peng Chau, and comes with a handy guidebook. Another time-saving option is the HKTB's Lantau Island tour, which takes in the monastery and Big Buddha, Cheung Sha Beach and the stilted fishing village of Tai O, home to the *Tanka* boat people.

More adventurous islandhoppers can find various ferry and *kaido* services that will enable them to explore more of Hong Kong's backwater villages, such as the fishing communities of Tap Mun (accessible via Tolo Harbour or Sai Kung) or Po Toi (via Stanley or Aberdeen).

A–Z

In the following section the city's attractions and services are organized by theme, under alphabetical headings. Items that link to another theme are cross-referenced. All sights that are plotted on the atlas section at the end of the book are given a page number and grid reference.

Architecture

A forest of gleaming towers, Hong Kong's cityscape is a dazzling emblem of its energy and role as a regional financial centre, and Hong Kong has become a centre of modern architecture. Building continues apace – as it has done since the 1980s, drawing the world's star architects, who have come here to realise some of their most ambitious ideas, in glass, steel and rarer materials. Many older buildings were swept away in the push for modernisation, but there's a new interest in conserving Hong Kong's heritage so a few historic treasures are here to be discovered.

Colonial Hong Kong

The British administrators of Hong Kong began putting up buildings in styles to their taste soon after the foundation of the colony in 1841. The first settlement was around Possession Street in Sheung Wan, but the centre of administration was on higher, more salubrious ground further east, which became known as **Government Hill**.

The city's first Anglican church, the neo-Gothic **St John's Cathedral**, was inaugurated there in 1849. The army headquarters, **Flagstaff House** (1846), and **Government House**, the official residence of Hong Kong's governors (1855), on the other hand, were both built in neoclassical style.

SEE ALSO MUSEUMS AND GALLERIES, P.64, TEMPLES AND HISTORIC SITES, P.114

1920s–1930s

Hong Kong experienced its first big burst of growth after World War I, but few major buildings from that era remain. The most distinguished survivor is **The Peninsula** hotel,

from 1928, though its 30-storey central tower was only added in the 1990s. Hong Kong's first skyscraper came in 1935 at **Chater Garden**, on Statue Square (Central). The sombre granite building has been demolished, leaving a pair of bronze lions marking the spot at the foot of its replacement, the HSBC head-quarters *(see opposite)*.

SEE ALSO HOTELS, P.60

1945–1980

The growth of Hong Kong really soared with the massive population influx from mainland China after the Communist takeover in 1949, and thousands lived in 'squatter huts', effectively shanty towns. In reaction to a disastrous fire in 1953 that made 50,000 homeless, the government embarked on a massive public housing policy, building functional housing estates then later developing the high-rise new towns in the New Territories. This era saw the demolition of colonial landmarks such as the original 1920s Repulse Bay Hotel and Kowloon Canton Railway

When Hong Kong's airport was at nearby Kai Tak, official restrictions limited the height of all buildings in Kowloon. Since the new airport opened in 1998, though, Kowloon has become the new area for developers to realise their most ambitious projects. In 2005 the Langham Place shopping mall, hotel and office complex kick-started regeneration in Mong Kok. Kowloon's mushrooming structures also include Hong Kong's first solar-powered skyscraper, One Peking Road, and The Masterpiece containing the K-11 mall and Hong Kong's tallest building, the 118-storey International Commerce Centre above Kowloon MTR station.

Station on the TST waterfront.

In 1973 Hong Kong's first modern office tower, the 50-storey, aluminium-clad **Jardine House**, was built for Jardine Matheson, one of the colony's oldest companies. It was surpassed by the circular **Hopewell Centre** in 1980.

Jardine House
1 Connaught Place, Central;
MTR: Central; map p.137 D3

Left: steel and glass symbolise Hong Kong's modern skyline.

Hong Kong's heritage, and battles between conservationists and developers. Early 20th century Chinese *tong lau* shophouses are being preserved in Wan Chai and Kowloon and the government is seeking new uses for listed-buildings.

More usual for Hong Kong is the 2003 **International Financial Centre Two (Two IFC)** tower, at 415m (1,362ft), capped by curving spires and its 'partner' across the harbour **International Commerce Centre** (ICC) at 484m (1,588ft). The observation deck, **Sky100** (www.sky 100.com.hk; daily 10am–10pm, admission charge) on the 100th floor of ICC provides a bird's-eye view of the latest building works in progress.

In 2012, **Opus** (www.opus hongkongcom), a stunning Frank Gehry-designed tower on Stubbs Road, became the most expensive piece of residential real estate in town.

Two IFC
8 Finance Street, Central; MTR: Central; map p.137 D4
ICC
1 Austin Road West, Kowloon; MTR: Kowloon; map p.134 A4

1981–1999

Hong Kong surged skywards with a string of emblematic buildings. The **HSBC Main Building** designed by Norman Foster was completed in 1986, With its distinctive structure and vast atrium open to the public, 'The Bank' is a symbol of modern Hong Kong. In 1988, the **Lippo Centre** at Admiralty opened.

In 1990 the HSBC was joined by the equally spectacular, bamboo-inspired **Bank of China** tower by I.M. Pei.

In Wan Chai **Central Plaza**, Hong Kong's third-tallest structure with 78 storeys, opened in 1992, and the bird-like **Peak Tower**, by British architect Terry Farrell, in 1996.

The last years of the century saw a wave of new infrastructure projects. The **Hong Kong Convention and Exhibition Centre**, begun in 1994, was completed just in time to host the Handover ceremony in 1997. In May 1997 the 2.5km (1½-mile) **Tsing Ma Bridge** opened, linking the city to Lantau and the new airport. The vast new **Hong Kong International Airport**, opened in 1998 at Chek Lap Kok on reclaimed land off Lantau. In the same year the 346m (1,135ft) high **The Center** tower rose above Sheung Wan, and still stuns the city with its nightly light display.

Bank of China
1 Garden Road, Central; viewing gallery Mon–Fri 8am–6pm; MTR: Central; map p.137 D2
The Center
99 Queen's Road, Western; MTR: Central; map p.137 C3
Central Plaza
18 Harbour Road, Wan Chai; MTR: Wan Chai; map p.138 B3
Hong Kong Convention and Exhibition Centre
1 Expo Drive, Wan Chai; MTR: Wan Chai; map p.138 A3
HSBC Main Building
1 Queen's Road, Central; MTR: Central; map p.137 D2
Lippo Centre
89 Queensway, Central; MTR: Admiralty; map p.137 E2
Peak Tower
128 Peak Road, Central; daily 7am–midnight; Peak Tram: Garden Road; map p.136 C1

Post-Millennium

The new millennium saw nascent interest in preserving

Below: Bank of China.

Bars and Cafés

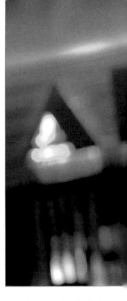

Take in the local scene at Hong Kong's growing number of cafés. WiFi is often available and tea and coffee specialists are the latest thing. For the ultimate authentic Hong Kong café pop in a *cha chaan teng*. For something more indulgent, linger over a British style afternoon tea at a five-star Hong Kong hotel. If you fancy something stronger, there are a huge number of bars open all hours. Lan Kwai Fong attracts the younger crowd, and visitors can mingle with an international after-work crowd there and around SoHo (south of Hollywood Road). In Tsim Sha Tsui, Knutsford Terrace is a good starting place.

Central, the Peak and Western

Al's Diner
27–39 D'Aguilar Street, Lan Kwai Fong; tel: 2869 1869; daily 11.30am–12.30am; MTR: Central (exit D1, D2), bus: 12M, 13, 23A, 40M; map p.137 C3

A pioneer of the Lan Kwai Fong area. Stop by for a slice of Americana and try their famous vodka Jello shots and check out The Fong.

Barista Jam
126–128 Jervois Street, Sheung Wan; tel: 2854 2211; www.baristajam.com.hk; Mon 10am–6pm, Tue–Fri 8am–6pm, Sat–Sun 10am–6pm; MTR Sheung Wan; map p.136 B3

Funky little café for coffee aficionados in cool two-floor venue. Seating is shared benches in post-industrial steely interior and wi-fi available. Snacks and light meals also served, in addition to great coffee.

Club 1911
G/F 27 Staunton Street, SoHo, Central; tel: 2810 6681; Sun–Fri 5pm–1am, Fri–Sat 5pm–2am; MTR: Central (exit D1, D2), bus: 12M, 13, 23A, 40M; map p.136 B3

Named after the year revolution overthrew the Qing dynasty in China, this cosy bar is decorated with vintage Chinese and Western images from the era. Join the workers on their way home for the daily happy hour 5–9pm.

Fotogallerie
2/F Fringe Club, 2 Lower Albert

Cocktails *(left)* are often a better bet in Hong Kong than straight spirits if you are looking for more of a bang for your buck. You get two or three shots per glass for not much extra cost, and in the best Hong Kong bars cocktails are expertly put together.

Road, Central; tel: 2521 7251; www.hkfringe.com.hk; daily noon–late; MTR: Central; map p.137 C2

Situated between the theatre and galleries and the roof top bar, this café gallery is a find. Its lunchtime veggie buffets are packed otherwise you can grab a coffee or drink, plus tapas and snacks through the day and check out the latest photography exhibition.

The Globe
45–53 Graham Street, Central; tel: 2543 1941; daily 10am–2am; MTR: Central (exit D1, D2), bus: 12M, 13, 23A, 40M; map p.136 B3

Vast English-style gastropub, The Globe has one of the best selections of beers in town with over a dozen beers on draught and a long list of obscure and well-known bottled beers to sample. Food is pretty good, but this is not the place for a quiet meal.

Holly Brown
22 Stanley Street, Central; tel: 2869 9008; www.hollybrown coffee.com; Mon–Fri 7.30am–midnight, Sat 8am–midnight, Sun 9am–10pm; MTR: Central; map p.137 C3

Wine

Hong Kong is Asia's wine-drinking capital *(left)*, and since scrapping the sales tax on wine it is the regional hub for the wine trade wine has become a fashionable drink. French wines are especially revered, and most bars offer a choice of Old and New World red and white wines by the glass.

daily, 4.30–8pm. Popular for people-watching after work, La Dolce Vita is buzzing all night.

Le Jardin

1/F, 10 Wing Wah Lane, Central; tel: 2526 2717; Mon–Wed noon–1am, Fri–Sat noon–3am; MTR: Central (exit D1, D2), bus: 12M, 13, 23A, 26, 40M; map p.137 C3

Outdoor bar in the Central and Lan Kwai Fong area, half-hidden up some steps at the end of a winding lane. Isolation from the bustle below encourages a laid-back mood, drawing a pleasant, mixed crowd, and there is great jukebox music as well as fascinating views over the frenzy of pavement restaurants below, all from the comfort of a roof terrace.

Linq

35 Pottinger Street, SoHo, Central; tel: 2971 0680 MTR: Central; Mon–Thur 5pm–2am, Fri–Sat 5pm–late; map p.137 C3

Most Hong Kong bars have long Happy Hours, with discounts of up to 30 percent, or special promotions, such as two drinks for the price of one. Happy Hours usually run during the early evenings, but can be at any time of the day, so plan ahead and you should find somewhere to fit your timetable. Some bars also offer free drinks for women on certain nights. Check with bar staff before ordering, as some locations have different policies for which drinks are included in their Happy Hour offers.

Now the upmarket boutiques are moving up Stanley Street, shoppers have a place to go for a latte or homemade gelato. Cup-cake desserts or light meals also available. Additional branch in K-11, TST.

Knockbox

Shop B, 14 Tai Ping Shan Street, Sheung Wan; daily – variable times; MTR: Sheung Wan; map p.136 B3

A tiny coffee shop tucked away off trendy Tai Ping Shan Street, if you obsess about coffee, seek out Knockbox. Laboratory-like equipment allows the passionate coffee-loving owners and baristas to perfect their brews. Regular tastings and guest beans.

La Dolce Vita 97

Cosmos Building, 9–11 Lan Kwai Fong, Central; tel: 2186 1888; Mon–Thur noon–2am, Fri noon–3am, Sat 2pm–3am, Sun 2pm–2am; MTR: Central (exit D1, D2), bus: 12M, 12, 23A, 26, 40M; map p.137 C3

Funky, open-fronted Italian café-bar with pulsating post-house music and tasty Italian snacks, and Happy Hours

Right: Central's stylish clientele and surroundings.

Above: enjoying a drink in one of the bars in Hollywood Road.

Linq is a long but cosy Bohemian bar opening on to the stone steps of Pottinger Street. Slip inside for a quiet drink by candlelight or grab a spot by the door for some people-watching.

Oolaa

G/F Centre Stage, Bridges Street, Sheung Wan; tel: 2803 2083; daily 7.30am–late; MTR: Central, Sheung Wan; map p.136 B3

An all-day dining destination, Oolaa's location in up and coming area, provides a vast (for Hong Kong) space. There is café seating with newspa-

pers and magazines, plus an open-fronted restaurant and a lounge bar. Vibe is laid back urban Australian and the vast menu of international dishes shows food and drink are taken seriously.

Pier 7 Café & Bar

Roof Viewing Deck, Central Pier 7, Star Ferry, Central; tel: 2167 8377; daily 9am–midnight; MTR: Central; map p.137 D4

Classy place to stop by for a coffee or beverage break at the Central Star Ferry Pier, with outdoor deck. Stay for happy hour and watch the city light up.

Starbucks

Floor M2, Baskerville House, 13 Duddell Street, Central; tel: 2523 5685; www.starbucks.com.hk; Mon–Fri 7am–9pm, Sat 8am–10pm, Sun 9am–8pm; MTR: Central; map p.137 C2

If you need your fix of Starbucks, or you like vintage interiors, try this refreshingly individual retro Starbucks. The café serves all the usual menu and in the rear half you catch a glimpse of old-style Hong Kong's *bing sutt* (Ice Room), which was a cool place to hang out in the 50s and 60s.

Staunton's

10 Staunton Street, Central; tel: 2973 6611; daily 10am–2am; Central-Mid-Levels Escalator,

bus: 12M, 13, 23A, 26, 40M; map p.136 B3

Stauntons is easy to find – on a corner right next to the Central-Mid-Levels Escalator, making it a popular place to meet up. Upstairs seating and balcony is ideal for weekend brunches.

Tastings Wine Bar

Basement, 27–29 Wellington Street, Central; tel: 2523 6282; Mon–Sat 5pm–2am; MTR: Central; map p.136 C3

A sophisticated wine bar offering over 160 different wines from around the world. Choose between a 25ml taste, half glass or full glass of more than 40 wines by the glass.

Tsui Wah

G/F–2/F, 15–19 Wellington Street, Central; tel: 2525 6338; daily 24 hours; MTR Central; map p.137 C3

Loud, bright and always open, Tsui Wah is the best-known *cha chaan teng* in town. From office workers and school kids during the day to bar flies and celebs in the wee small hours, you can always find something filling to eat here. Lots of quirky Hong Kong-style tea, coffee and iced drinks.

V13-Vodka Bar

13 Old Bailey Street; daily 5pm–2am; Central-Mid-Levels Escalator, bus: 12M, 13, 23A, 26,

---

Karaoke has been serious fun in Hong Kong since the 1980s; any number of bars and even some restaurants have 'karaoke boxes' for crooners' privacy. The boxes are dotted all over town, but particularly numerous around Causeway Bay. They are very popular at weekends, but rental fees and drinks can be pricey, and booking ahead is advisable at peak times. Many establishments don't have the songs or the language skills to deal with non-Chinese singers. The citywide Neway chain is one of the best, and the most foreigner-friendly one is CEO Neway, 2–8 Sugar Street, Causeway Bay, tel: 2196 2196; MTR: Causeway Bay (exit E).

40M; map p.136 B3

True to its name, there is a lot of vodka here, but there's also plenty of cold beers, creative cocktails and wine by the glass. Overlooking the historic former Central Police Station, V13 also has live music weekly and a decent playlist at other times.

Wan Chai and Causeway Bay

1/5 Nuevo

Starcrest, 9 Star Street, Wan Chai; tel: 2529 2300; Mon–Sat noon–late, Sun 5pm–late; bus: 5, 5A, 10; map p.138 A2

The name of this loft-style bar is pronounced 'One Fifth' by those in the know. The clientele is exclusive and glamorous; get there early to grab a booth, and dress in your finest gear to get in at all.

Agave

93 Lockhart Road, Wan Chai; tel: 2866 3228; Sun–Thur noon–2am, Fri–Sat noon–4am; MTR: Wan Chai (exit C1); bus: Gloucester and Hennessy roads; map p.138 A2

Lively place, serving margaritas, over 160 varieties of tequila (possibly the biggest range in Asia) and possibly the world.

Carnegies

53–55 Lockhart Road, Wan Chai; tel: 2866 6289; daily noon–2am;

Beer-drinking will be more enjoyable if you try locally brewed labels, such as Chinese Tsing Tao, instead of the more instantly recognisable world-wide brands (some of which are notorious for giving worse hangovers in the humid tropics).

MTR: Wan Chai (exit A1, C), bus: Gloucester and Hennessy roads; map p.138 A2

Friendly, laid-back and very popular bar with American and Asian snacks, a lively clientele and plenty of good, old-fashioned American-style fun. Where else can you dance on the bar top?

Delaney's

G–1/F, One Capital Place, 18 Luard Road, Wan Chai; tel: 2804 2880; daily noon–2am, Fri–Sat until 3am; MTR: Wan Chai (exit A1, C); bus: Gloucester and Hennessy roads; map p.138 A3

Very popular Irish theme pub, serving (very pricey) Guinness and good food, at better-value prices. A giant screen upstairs shows rugby and football matches; there is a less packed bar downstairs. Another branch is at 71–7 Peking Road, Tsim Sha Tsui (tel: 2301 3980).

Dusk till Dawn

74–84 Jaffe Road, Wan Chai; tel: 2528 4689; Mon–Fri noon–

6am, Sat–Sun 3pm–6am; MTR: Wan Chai (exit A1, C), bus: Gloucester and Hennessy roads; map p.138 A3

A lively, often packed fun bar where expats let their hair down to sounds provided by an excellent live Filipino cover band.

East End Brewery

Sunning Plaza, 10 Hysan Avenue, Causeway Bay; tel: 2577 9119; daily 11.30am–1am, Fri–Sat until 1.30am; MTR: Causeway Bay (exit F); map p.139 D2

Casual, patio-style bar with good selection of beers, including some imported from microbreweries. The covered terrace, popular on warm evenings, is shared with adjacent Inn Side Out.

Mes Amis

83 Lockhart Road, Wan Chai; tel: 2527 6680; daily noon–1am, Fri–Sat until 2am; MTR: Wan Chai (exit A1, C), bus: Gloucester and Hennessy roads; map p.138 A2

This French wine bar in the heart of clubland has a good list of wines and Mediterranean-style snacks. Turns into a wild-ish dance joint after 10pm on Friday and Saturday, with DJs. Slightly calmer branches in 5 Ashley Road, TST; tel 2730 3038 and 13/F Langham Place, Mong Kok; tel: 3428 3699.

Below: a Hong Kong branch of the ever-popular Starbucks coffee chain.

City-Wide Caffeine

As well as international branded coffee chains, Hong Kong has a few homegrown chains offering comfy chairs and an enticing menu of coffee, blended drinks, snacks and free wi-fi. The largest is Pacifc Coffee and fresh and airy boutique chain Caffe Habittu is worth checking out too.What claims to be Hong Kong's first coffee shop – Uncle Russ Coffee (Pier 3 and 5 Central Piers, TST Star Ferry Pier) is good for coffee on the run.

Tea set time

All kinds of small cafés in Hong Kong offer an "afternoon tea set" after the queue-loving lunchtime office crowds subside around 2–4pm. The name and timing is inspired by the British tradition, but typically a "tea set" is a small portion of the outlets' specialities, served with a choice of coffee, tea or a soft drink. If you can miss the crowds, and need to duck for cover from the sun or rain it can be a good value late lunch.

Above: a traditional serving of tea.

The Pawn

62 Johnston Road, Wan Chai; tel: 2866 3444; daily 11am–2am, Sun 11am–midnight; MTR: Wan Chai (exit B1); bus 1, 11, 25; map p.139 A2

A restored 19th century pawnshop, transformed into one of Wan Chai's coolest bars and restaurants. Pull up a rattan lounge chair on the balcony, order some excellent gastro-pub fare and watch the trams, the world and Wan Chai go by.

World Peace Café

21–23 Tai Wong Street East, Wan Chai; tel: 2527 5870; Mon–Sat noon–3pm, Fri–Sat 6.30–9.30pm; MTR: Wan Chai, bus: 109, 111; map p138 A2

This organic and vegetarian café run by a Buddhist organisation doubles as a meditation centre, and is largely staffed by volunteers. Stop by for juices and smoothies, fairtrade coffee and speciality herbal teas.

The Southside

Beaches

92B Stanley Main Street, Stanley; tel: 2813 7313; Mon–Fri 9am–midnight, Sat–Sun 9am–1am; bus: 6, 260, 973

At weekends, Stanley's main street is packed with families, tourists and young couples. There are heaps of watering

holes along this stretch of road catering to the crowds, but Beaches is the best of the bunch. A good place for a light nibble and a beverage or two.

The Smuggler's Inn

90A Main Street, Stanley; tel: 2813 8852; Mon–Fri 9am–midnight, Sat–Sun 9am–1am; bus: 6, 260, 973

This British-style pub is a throwback to the pre-97 era, when army boys came here from Stanley Fort to spend half their wages. It still feels like it is stuck back in the days when Britain held all the pink bits on the world map.

Kowloon

18 Grams

B04, 56 Dundas Street, Gala Place Basement, Mong Kok; tel: 2770 1339; daily 11.30am–9.30pm; MTR: Yau Ma Tei; map p.132 B2

18 Grams is a prime example of Hong Kong's new independent cafés. With the emphasis on fresh, locally-roasted coffee beans, the café offers espresso-based coffee, of course with homemade desserts and a menu of light meals including pastas and all day Canadian and Australian breakfasts. Other branches can be found in: **Gateway Arcade, Harbour City TST** and **15 Canon Street, Causeway Bay.**

Agnès b Café

G28 K11, 18 Hanoi Road, Tsim Sha Tsui; tel: 3122 4184; daily 10am–10pm; MTR: Tsim Sha Tsui, East Tsim Sha Tsui; map p.134 C2

Oh so cool Agnès b café's ooze European charm and have popped up all over Hong Kong. A high-profile sponsor of the arts in Hong Kong, Agnès b cafés are a huge success. The K-11 branch has lovely glass windows to spy on passersby heading to the Art Mall. Serves up sandwiches, quiches and soups.

Bahama Mama's

4–5 Knutsford Terrace, Tsim Sha Tsui; tel: 2368 2121; Mon–Thur 3.30pm–3am, Fri–Sat 3.30pm–4am, Sun 4pm–2am; MTR: Tsim Sha Tsui (exit B2); bus: Nathan and Chatham roads; map p.134 C3

Long-established Caribbean-inspired theme bar with an unusual mix of front terrace, a dance floor where you can sway to reggae and funk beats, and table football for the non-rhythmic lads.

Charlie Brown Café

58–60 Cameron Road, Tsim Sha Tsui; tel: 2366 6315; Sun–Thur 8.30am–11pm, Fri–Sat 8.30am–midnight; MTR: Tsim Sha Tsui; map p.135 C2

For lovers of all things Peanuts and Italian coffee.

Original Fusion

Hong Kong's unique style of café is the *cha chaan teng*, which originated to fill the need for quick fast meals for busy factory or office workers in the 60s and 70s. Meaning a tea meal room, *cha chaan teng* serve a genuine fusion cuisine of Western elements such as individual servings and ingredients and Chinese food. Macaroni appears in soup, bread is used for giant doorstep egg or luncheon meat sandwiches and French toast. Tea and coffee is served hot and strong here, often with evaporated milk. At the most traditional *cha chaan tengs*, 'silk stocking tea' is strained as its name suggests. There are also plenty of rice or noodle meals among the value for money "meal sets". HK takes on Western drinks include yuanyuan a half and half mix of tea and coffee, iced ovaltine and some excellent iced coffee and iced lemon teas.

There are items aimed at kids but this is also a late night café too for young people. Snoopy's sitting on a stool, there are cakes in the shape of Linus, Lucy and Woodstock. Food menu includes burgers and sandwiches and reasonable meal sets.

Eyebar
30/F, iSQUARE, 63 Nathan Road, Tsim Sha Tsui; tel: 2487 3688; daily 11.30pm–late; MTR: Kowloon, Tsim Sha Tsui; map p.134 B2

One of the new generation of Kowloon bars that finally make the most of the stunning skyline that surround. Here there are floor-to ceiling windows and a harbour-facing terrace. The Eyebar happy hour deals are usually later rather than earlier for the after-dinner crowd.

Living Room
W Hong Kong, 1 Austin Road West, Kowloon Station; tel: 3717 2222; www.starwoodhotels.com; daily 7.30am–1am; MTR: Kowloon, Tsim Sha Tsui; map p.134 A3

The ICC, Elements and around Kowloon Station has added some stylish venues to the scene on the 'darkside'. The Living Room is often packed with a crowd who take advantage of the bar's selection of board games and signature cocktails.

Mariners' Rest
Hullett House, 2a Canton Road, Tsim Sha Tsui; tel: 3988 0103; daily 11am–11pm; MTR: Tsim Sha Tsui; Star Ferry

Take a tot of rum or a glass of beer and enjoy the authentic old-world ambience of this former police drinking den that must have seen their fair share of drunken sailors. Gastro-pub fare available.

Ozone
The Ritz-Carlton, Hong Kong, 118/F, ICC, 1 Austin Road West, Kowloon, tel: 2263 2263; Sun–Thur 5pm–1am, Fri 5pm–2am, Sat 4pm–2am, Sun noon–3pm; MTR: Kowloon; map p.134 A3

The highest bar in the world, Ozone is on the top floor of the Ritz-Carlton. Dress code means you must leave beachwear and flip-flops behind so dress to impress. You can enjoy the ultimate harbour view in Hong Kong from the outdoor terrace. Invest in some signature cocktails and Asian tapas to make the most of the location.

The New Territories

Jaspas Sai Kung
G/F 13A Sha Tsui Path Sai Kung; tel: 2792 6388; daily 8am–11pm; MTR Choi Hung, Minibus 1A or MTR Diamond Hill; bus: 92

Plenty of al fresco seating at this popular Sai Kung bar and restaurant with an Australian outdoor lifestyle vibe. Order a jug of cocktails or your favourite chilled beverage and try their excellent salads and platters.

The Outer Islands

The Waterfront
58 Yung Shue Wan Main Street, Lamma; tel: 2982 1168; daily 11am–late

Five minutes from the ferry pier, just off Lamma's main street, The Waterfront offers tasty fare from around the globe. The views make this one of the most pleasant places to take in the sunset in Hong Kong, especially after a hike.

Below: crowds spill onto the street on sultry summer nights.

Children

A lthough Hong Kong's family-friendly appeal is not immediately obvious, the city has a surprising amount of affordable and accessible attractions to offer inquisitive and active children. Besides amusement parks, hands-on museums, cable-car rides, nature activities and gadgets galore, the city's ferry and tram rides are sure to provide ample entertainment to any youngster, and curious kids should find many hidden treasures in the city's markets. Events and a raft of colourful festivals are held throughout the year, and the annual Hong Kong WinterFest lets children enjoy the Christmas season in the sun.

Hong Kong Disneyland

Lantau Island; tel: 1-830 830; www.hongkongdisneyland.com; hours vary, usually Apr–Oct: Sun–Thur 10.30am–8pm, Fri–Sat 10.30am–9pm, Nov–Mar: daily 10.30am–7.30pm; entrance charge; MTR: Sunny Bay, then change to special Resort trains
The magic begins on board the dedicated Disney Train (a Disney first), which passengers join at Sunny Bay station. Once inside the park kids will find all the old favourites, including Broadway-style shows, white-knuckle rides, Main Street USA, Toy Story Land, Fantasyland, Adventureland and Tomorrowland, along with fireworks displays and parades. Rides include the classic Disney attraction 'It's a Small World' and the interactive Muppet Mobile Lab hosted by the always unsuccessful Dr Bunsen.

Hong Kong Wetland Park

Wetland Park Road, Tin Shui Wai, New Territories; tel: 2708 8885; www.wetlandpark.com; Wed–Mon 10am–5pm; entrance charge; LRT: Wetland Park; bus: 967 from Admiralty

As well as offering an insight into Hong Kong's wetland reserve, a trip to this major attraction, in the northwestern New Territories, offers the chance to visit a part of Hong Kong that is a world away from the tourist centres. The park itself borders Mai Po and Deep Bay, and contains extensive wetland habitats. Access to birdwatching hides is provided via an extensive network of boardwalks. An impressive 10,000 sq m (108,000 sq ft) visitor centre features interactive exhibits.

Ngong Ping 360

11 Tat Tung Road, Lantau Island; tel: 2109 9898; www.np360. com.hk; Mon–Fri 10am–6pm, Sat–Sun 9am–6.30pm; entrance charge; MTR: Tung Chung
This 5.7km (3½-mile) Skyrail ride links Tung Chung with Lantau's **Po Lin Monastery** and takes in spectacular panoramic views of the South China Sea and North Lantau Country Park, as well as the monastery and its famous **Big Buddha** statue. On arrival at Ngong Ping village families will find several

Above: friendly faces at Ocean Park.

themed attractions including Walking with Buddha, the Monkey's Tale Theatre and Ngong Ping Tea House.
SEE ALSO TEMPLES AND HISTORIC SIGHTS, P.117

Ocean Park

Ocean Park Road, Aberdeen; tel: 3923 2323; www.oceanpark. com.hk; Mon–Sat 10.30am–7.30pm, Sun 9.30am–7.30pm; entrance charge; MTR: Admiralty, then Citybus: 629
One of Hong Kong's best-loved family attractions,

Left: visitors at Tomorrowland in Hong Kong Disneyland.

The Peak

Hong Kong Island; www.the peak.com.hk; daily 7am–midnight; Peak Tram: Garden Road; map p.136 B1
EA Experience: tel: 2849 7710; www.eaexperience.com; Mon–Fri noon–10pm, Sat–Sun 10am–10pm; entrance charge
Madame Tussaud's: tel: 2849 6966; www.madametussauds.com.hk; daily 10am–10pm; entrance charge

Half the fun of The Peak is in the getting there. Kids will love the clanky funicular or Peak Tram (in service since 1888), which climbs 373m (1,224 ft) at a white-knuckle, see-it-to-believe-it incline. The revamped **Peak Tower** now offers a 360-degree rooftop platform to take in the famously breathtaking view; while an expanded **Madame Tussaud's** features more than 100 wax models that include Hong Kong favourites Bruce Lee and Jackie Chan as well as David Beckham. The Peak also houses the **EA Experience**, with utterly state-of-the-art motion simulators and other virtual rides and games, plus acres of retail and dining space.

SEE ALSO TRANSPORT, P.123; WALKS AND VIEWS, P.126

The Pearl River Delta between Hong Kong and Macau is home to an estimated 1,000 Indo-Pacific humpback dolphins, known as *sousa chinensis*. **Hong Kong Dolphinwatch** (tel: 2984 1414; www.hkdolphin watch.com) runs trips to see the dolphins in their natural habitat off Lantau Island. If you do not spot one the first time you are entitled to go again free (Wed, Fri and Sun; adults HK$380, children HK$190).

Ocean Park – one of Asia's largest aquariums and marine-life theme parks – has lost none of its appeal.

As well as its reef-themed aquarium with dramatic shark tunnel and 'areas' including Amazing Asian Animals, Marine World, Whiskers Harbour, Rainforest and Thrill Mountain, the park also features a handful of stomach-churning rides including the Abyss Turbo Drop, and the Mine Train and Dragon roller-coasters. Responding to Hong Kong's new love of nostalgia, Ocean Park opened Old Hong Kong Street to celebrate its 35th anniversary in 2012. A must is a ride on the park's much-loved cable car, which hugs the coast of Aberdeen.

Below: fabulous jellyfish illuminate Ocean Park's Sea Jelly Aquarium.

Essentials

Finding your way around an unknown city can be quite daunting, but Hong Kong is so international and geared towards visitors that it is usually easy to get around and find information. Most hotel reception staff will usually help with communication problems and bookings. This section gives you the basic, most useful facts, from timing your trip to avoid the summer rainy season to finding the nearest hospital. For specific practical information on getting around Hong Kong see *Transport, p.118–25*, and see *Language, p.62–3*, for some basic phrases useful for travellers.

Baggage Restrictions

Since March 2007 revised restrictions apply on all flights into and out of Hong Kong (including passengers in transit) to the way in which liquids, gels and aerosols can be carried onto a plane. They must be in containers no bigger than 100ml, and placed in a single (maximum one per passenger) transparent resealable bag, with a capacity not exceeding 1litre.

Climate

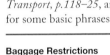

Hong Kong has a subtropical climate divided into four seasons:

Winter: Between late December and February, the weather generally varies from mild to cool, with some fog and rain. Temperatures average between 13°C and 20°C (55–68°F). However, they can occasionally dip down to below 10°C (50°F).

Spring: March to mid-May sees plenty of damp, overcast weather, but also pleasant sunny days. Temperatures range from a daytime average of 20°C (68°F) in March to 28°C (82°F) in May.

Summer: Temperatures and humidity rise to near-unbearable levels from late May to mid-September. Skies are intermittently clear, but usually hazy. Temperatures usually rise to 32°C (90°F) in the afternoon, with very high humidity. Thunderstorms are common. July–September is peak typhoon season.

Autumn: The northeast monsoon usually takes over by October, bringing cooler, drier air. From late September to late December expect clear blue skies and pleasant tem-

peratures, dropping from 29°C (84°F) at the end of September to around 20°C (68°F) in December. Humidity is generally quite low.

Consulates

Australia
Consulate-General, 23–24/F, Harbour Centre, 25 Harbour Road, Wan Chai; tel: 2827 8881; www.australia.org.hk; MTR: Wan Chai; map p.138 B3

Canada
Consulate-General, 11–14F, 1 Exchange Square, Central; tel: 3719 4700; www.hongkong.gc.ca; MTR: Central; map p.137 D3

New Zealand
Room 6501, Central Plaza, 18 Harbour Road, Wan Chai; tel: 2525 5044; www.nzembassy. com/hongkong; MTR: Wan Chai; map p.138 B3

Republic of Ireland
Honorary Consul, Heidrick & Struggles, Suite 1408, Two Pacific Place, 88 Queensway, Central; tel: 2527 4897; www.consulateofireland.hk; MTR: Admiralty; map p.137 D2

Left: hazy summer skies cover Two IFC.

Left: Hong Kong International Airport.

tem matches your requirements you have back home.

Emergencies and Police

Members of the Hong Kong Police Force wear navy-blue uniforms in winter and olive-green uniforms in summer. Many police officers speak English and are generally helpful. The police headquarters are located at Arsenal Street in Wan Chai; there are police stations and reporting centres throughout the territory, including in the Airport Express section of Hong Kong station in Central.

In an emergency dial **999**. To report crimes or make complaints call Hong Kong's Crime Hotline, tel: 2527 7177.

USEFUL NUMBERS
Emergency: 999 (police, fire, ambulance)
General Police Enquiries: 2527 7177
Hong Kong Immigration: 2824 6111 (24 hours)
Hospital Authority Helpline: 2300 6555
Department of Health: 2961 8989
Samaritans: 2896 0000

UK
Consulate-General, 1 Supreme Court Road, Central; tel: 2901 3000; http://ukinhongkong. fco.org.uk/en; MTR: Central; map p.137 E1
US
Consulate-General, 26 Garden Road, Central; tel: 2523 9011; http://hongkong.usconsulate.gov; MTR: Central; map p.137 D2

Customs

Hong Kong mostly lives up to its image of being a free port. Visitors aged 18 and above can import almost anything for their personal use (including an unlimited amount of cash), but only 19 cigarettes or 1 cigar or 25g of tobacco, and 1 litre of alcoholic liquor above 30 percent vol. There are no restrictions on wine and alcohol below 30 percent vol.

Firearms must be declared and handed over for safe-keeping until you depart. There are also stringent restrictions on the import and export of ivory and other items from the list of endangered species that are protected by CITES (Convention on International Trade in Endangered Species of Wild Fauna and Flora).

Electricity

Hong Kong's electrical system is rated at 200/220 volts and 50 cycles AC (alternating current). Most plug sockets take British-style three-pin plugs, but some take other types; usefully, the majority of hotels can supply all-purpose adaptors.

When purchasing electronics here, check that the sys-

Below: important directions are usually bilingual.

Above: Hong Kong dollars.

Health

You will have your temperature taken on arrival by automatic sensors when you pass through immigration, if it is high you will have a quick health check. This measure was introduced post-Sars. No vaccinations are required to enter Hong Kong, but it is advisable to have up-to-date immunisations against Hepatitis A and B, flu, polio and tetanus; if in doubt, check with your doctor or a travel health clinic before travelling.

Hong Kong's roadside pollution is extremely high at times and people with heart and respiratory problems should monitor air quality reports in newspapers and online. Visit the Environmental Protection Department; www.epd.gov.hk.

As of January 2007 Hong Kong went smoke-free. Smoking is now prohibited in most enclosed public places, including restaurants, karaoke bars, malls and some bars, as well as some outdoor areas (public beaches and swimming pools, transport interchanges and outside escalators).

Hong Kong also has strict laws to maintain environmental hygiene, including a fixed penalty fine of HK$1,500 for littering and spitting in public.

MEDICAL TREATMENT AND HOSPITALS

All visitors are strongly advised to take out adequate travel and health insurance before arriving in Hong Kong to cover medical emergencies, hospitalisation and all other possible medical expenses. Hong Kong does not have a free national health care system, and visitors are required to pay at least HK$570 if they use the Accident and Emergency services at Hong Kong's public hospitals.

Listed below are two of the hospitals that have 24-hour emergency services. For more information on all medical services, call the efficient Hospital Authority helpline, tel: 2300 6555, or visit www.ha.org.hk.

When to Visit

Weather-wise the ideal time to visit Hong Kong is October to December: warm, and with blue skies but low humidity. In January or February, Chinese New Year offers a spectacular celebration, but many places will be closed for the holiday. April to August, the rainy season, is generally the least pleasant time to sightsee.

Caritas Medical Centre
111 Wing Hong Street, Sham Sui Po, Kowloon; tel: 3408 7911; MTR: Sham Shui Po
Queen Mary Hospital
102 Pok Fu Lam Road, Pok Fu Lam, near Aberdeen, Southside, Hong Kong Island; tel: 2855 3838; bus: 3A, 3B, 40M, 91, M49

PHARMACIES

Conventional pharmacies (identified by a red-cross sign) are abundant in Hong Kong, as are traditional Chinese herbalists. Some pharmacies will only accept prescriptions issued by a doctor in Hong Kong.

Internet

Nearly all hotels will offer wi-fi or wired-in Broadband internet access. Free wi-fi 'hotspots' are common in major shopping malls and government buildings. You can also access the internet for free at computers in many coffee shops, large shopping malls, major MTR stations and public libraries.

Money

The currency unit is the Hong Kong dollar, pegged to the US dollar at a rate of roughly US$1: HK$7.75.

Banknotes are issued by Hongkong Shanghai Bank (HSBC), Standard Chartered Bank and the Bank of China in denominations of HK$1,000 (orange), HK$500 (brown), HK$100 (red), HK$50 (purple), HK$20 (grey-green, except for the Bank of China's, which are blue), and the new plasticised HK$10 (purple). Coins issued include HK$10, HK$5, HK$2, HK$1, 50 cents, 20 cents and 10 cents.

BANKS

Banking hours are Monday to Friday 9am–4.30pm, Saturday 9am–12.30pm. Licensed moneychangers and hotels are an alternative option, but they can sting you with a hefty service charge. Moneychangers in Tsim Sha Tsui, Causeway Bay and Wan Chai stay open until late at night.

CREDIT CARDS AND CHEQUES

Plastic is used with a vengeance in Hong Kong: Visa, MasterCard, American Express, Diners Club and other major cards are accepted at most hotels, restaurants and shops. However, be sure to check the cash price in shops; it may be lower than that for card sales. In most street markets only cash is accepted.

Cash machines (ATMs) can also be found everywhere. Visa and MasterCard holders can obtain local currency from Hang Seng Bank and Hongkong Shanghai Bank (HSBC) cash machines (ATMs); American Express cardholders can access Jetco ATMs.

Travellers' cheques are readily accepted by banks, hotels and moneychangers.

Post

The Hong Kong mail service is fast and efficient. Stamps normally have to be bought at post offices: most are

open Monday to Friday 9.30am–6pm, Saturday 9.30am–1pm. Two are open seven days a week, bar public holidays: the General Post Office, near IFC (2 Connaught Place, Central; Mon–Sat 8am–6pm, Sun 9am–5pm), and the TST Post Office (G/F, Hermes House, 10 Middle Road, Tsim Sha Tsui; Mon–Sat 9am–6pm, Sun 9am–2pm). For more information on all postal services, tel: 2921 2222; www.hongkong post.com.

Telephones

Public telephones are getting harder to find in Hong Kong, but the easiest places to find them are MTR stations, 7–11 stores, and hotel lobbies, where local calls will be free. Hotels will charge for all calls made from your hotel room.

Below: colonial remnants.

You can make international direct dial (IDD) calls from public card phones with a credit card or stored-value phone card (available at HKTB Information and Gift Centres, 7–11 stores and some bookshops). To make a call outside Hong Kong, first dial the international access code, **001**, followed by the country code and number. To call Hong Kong from abroad or mainland China, the code is **852**. Within Hong Kong, there are no area codes and all numbers have eight digits, except for toll-free numbers, which begin with **800**, and some public information numbers, which begin with **18** or **10**.

For mobile (cell) users, most of the telephone sys-

Above: gathering information at the Hong Kong Tourist Board.

tems used around the world, including GSM 900, PCS 1800, CDMA and WCDMA, operate in Hong Kong.

HK SIM CARDS
Buy pre-paid mobile phone Sim cards in 7–11 stores and at service provider stores. Major phone service providers in Hong Kong are CSL, PCCW, 3, China Mobile and Smartone.

USEFUL NUMBERS
Hong Kong Directory Enquiries: 1081
International Directory Enquiries: 10013
International Operator/ Reverse Charge (Collect) calls: 10010
Hong Kong International Airport Information, in English: 2181 0000 (24 hours)
Weather Information: 187 8066
News-Hourly Updates RTHK Newsline: 2272 0000

> Hong Kong residents are required to carry an identity card, and visitors are advised to carry a similar form of photo identification, such as a passport.

Time
Hong Kong is eight hours ahead of GMT and 13 hours ahead of US Eastern Standard Time. Unlike Europe and the US, there is no daylight saving time, so from April to October the difference is reduced to seven hours ahead of London and 12 hours ahead of New York.

Tipping
Most restaurants and hotels automatically add a 10 percent service charge to the total bill. It is still general practice to round up a restaurant bill to the nearest 10 (larger gratuities are expected when there is no service charge added to the bill), or a taxi fare to the nearest dollar or two. Toilet attendants and doormen can be tipped one or two dollars. HK$10–20 is about right for porters and room service in most hotels.

Tourist Information
The best Hong Kong Tourist Board (HKTB)) office to check out is located by Star Ferry pier in Tsim Sha Tsui, Kowloon. On arrival collect a free HKTB information bag in the baggage claim area at the airport, which contains a map, current events magazine, comprehensive brochures and details of day and half-day tours organised by HKTB.

The HKTB also has an information centre at the Peak Piazza, between the Peak Tower and the Peak Galleria.

There is also an excellent multilingual Visitor Hotline, tel: 2508 1234 (daily 9am–6pm), or for more information in advance visit www.discover hongkong.com.

Hong Kong International Airport
Transfer Area E2 and Buffer Halls A and B, Arrivals Level, Terminal 1; daily 7am–11pm
Hong Kong Island
The Peak Piazza; daily 9am–9pm; MTR; Central; map p.136 C1
Kowloon
Star Ferry Concourse, Tsim Sha Tsui; daily 8am–8pm; MTR: Tsim Sha Tsui; map p.134 B1

Above: the length of your tourist visa depends on where you come from.

Visas and Passports

Most visitors only need a valid passport to enter Hong Kong. The length of visa-free tourist visit that is allowed varies according to your nationality. British subjects holding full UK passports are granted six months on entry; all other European Union nationals get three months, as do most British dependent passport holders and nationals of Australia, Brazil, Brunei, Canada, Chile, Ecuador, Israel, Malaysia, New Zealand, Norway, Japan, Singapore, Switzerland, Turkey and the USA.

Citizens of other countries should consult the Chinese Embassy or Consulate-General in their country of origin, or visit the Hong Kong Immigration Department website, www.immd.gov.hk. All visitors should note that when they arrive their passport needs to be valid for at least one month beyond the planned date of departure from Hong Kong, or they may be refused entry.

Visas for travel to **mainland China** can be obtained when you are in Hong Kong. These require two photos and usually take about three working days to process, for around HK$200–300. Visas can be obtained from these offices, or from many Hong Kong travel agents:
China Travel Service
Tel: 2851 1700; www.ctshk.com
Has several branches around Hong Kong.
Visa Office of the People's Republic of China
7/F, Lower Block, China Resources Centre, 26 Harbour Road, Wan Chai; tel: 3413 2424; MTR: Wan Chai; map p.138 B3

What to Wear

Hong Kong is a much 'smarter' city than, say, Bangkok or Manila. Smart-casual attire will see you through most social occasions, outside of business (where suits and dresses are standard) or official functions. Some hotels, restaurants, bars and nightclubs will not admit patrons in trainers (sneakers), flip-flops (thongs), jeans or shorts, or collarless shirts (for men).

Left: tourist-friendly signs make Hong Kong easy to navigate.

Festivals

Despite its brash and modern exterior, Hong Kong's population remains firmly rooted in tradition. Temple deities and ancestors are honoured with equal fervour, and barely a month goes by when an ancient tradition or festival is not marked with a colourful pageant or celebratory meal. These traditions are at their most vibrant and visible during the exuberant Chinese New Year festival and the Mid-Autumn Festival with lanterns lighting up the sky. Here is only a sample of the many events that are celebrated throughout the year.

Chinese New Year
Late Jan or early Feb
Lunar New Year is Hong Kong's major annual event. Family is key to this festival.

Lunar New Year is the biggest festival of the year in Hong Kong. With three days of public holidays, all offices are closed and a few restau-

Below: the procession up the stairs at the Birthday of Lord Buddha Festival, Lin Po Monastery.

rants and stores close to let staff spend time with their families. But aside from the first day of the year, (the day for family meals), the city is buzzing. Most retailers are open and the city is colourfully decked out in lucky red and gold, orange trees and festive lights often in the shape of the New Year's animal.

Millions cross the border from the Mainland for their annual holiday and shopping too and many colourful events that take place either side of the huge New Year's Day parade. The parade, with its spectacular dragon dances and processions is a sight (and sound) to behold. Tourists can join locals at temples, flower markets, and on the waterfront for a spectacular firework display over Victoria Harbour on the second day of the New Year.

Cheung Chau Bun Festival
One week in late Apr or early May
One of Hong Kong's most exciting and peculiar festivals. During the eight-day spring festival the residents of Che-

Hong Kong Wine and Dine Festival is a gigantic wine and food tasting extravaganza held on the West Kowloon Waterfront Promenade. Showcasing wines and food from around the world, local restaurants and bars also participate. Visitors can buy special tasting passes to join in the wine tastings and themed pairings. The festival kicks off a citywide Hong Kong Wine and Dine Month, which runs from late October through November and includes promotions, wine events and street carnivals in Lan Kwai Fong and Stanley. Also in the autumn the Marco Polo Hongkong Hotel has the best Oktoberfest (www.gbfhk. com) in Asia. Nightly festivities in a marquee on the waterfront all month. German beer and food and oompah bands make for a hilarious cultural juxtaposition and fun night out.

ung Chau island try to dispel what are known as 'hungry ghosts'. Take a ferry to Cheung Chau and make your way along the harbour promenade to the Pak Tai Temple. Here,

Left: Cheung Chau's lucky Buns.

If you are keen to learn more about Hong Kong's festivals, you can join a Festival Tour. These include Dragon Boat Festival Tours, a Chinese New Year Fireworks Cruise, Cheung Chau Bun Festival tours, a mid-Autumn Moonlight Cruise, and Buddha and Tin Hau Festival tours. Tours include such things as reserved seats at processions, meals, martial arts demonstrations and transport, such as ferries. For details of upcoming tours, enquire at tourist offices, or check www.discoverhongkong.com.

18m (60ft) high bamboo towers filled with buns are erected as offerings to the ghosts, and a spectacular float procession winds through the streets with children, richly costumed as figures from Chinese myths, 'floating' above the heads of the adults dressed as Taoist priests, suspended by means of hidden supports.
SEE ALSO OUTER ISLANDS, P.20

Birthday of Lord Buddha
Late Apr, early May
The devout celebrate the birthday of the Lord Buddha (Fourth Moon) with a ritual bathing of the Buddha on the outlying island of Lantau, where the famous **Big Buddha** is located within **Po Lin Monastery**. But, if you cannot make it to Lantau, celebrations take place at all Hong Kong's major temples and monasteries, where worshippers bathe Buddha statues. Interested visitors can also observe special ceremonies at Miu Fat Monastery near Tuen Mun.
SEE ALSO TEMPLES AND HISTORIC SITES, P.117

Dragon Boat Festival
June
The *Tuen Ng* or Dragon Boat Festival is second only to Chinese New Year in terms of pageantry and spectacle, and, as well as being great fun to watch, is one the few festivals in which locals and expats get together to have fun and let their hair down. The event combines a tradi-

Chinese festivals operate according to the lunar calendar, so their dates in the Western calendar vary from year to year. Beginning with Chinese New Year in late January or early February, the year is divided into 12 months of 29 days, with an extra month added every two and a half years, similar to our leap years. The calendar operates in 60-year cycles, divided into five smaller cycles of 12 years. Each lunar year is represented by an animal, and, as in Western astrology, the permutations – rat, ox, tiger, rabbit, dragon, snake, horse, ram, monkey, rooster, dog and pig – are thought to provide clues into a person's character.

tional celebration with thrilling races, held at various venues around Hong Kong. Teams of paddlers practise in earnest for months before the event, when they race in elaborately decorated narrow dragon boats sporting dragon's heads and tails to the beat of loud onboard drums. International dragon-boat races are held in the following month.
SEE ALSO SPORT, P.111

Mid-Autumn Festival
Late Sept or Oct
This is one of Hong Kong's most popular festivals. Also known as the Moon Festival (it celebrates the full harvest moon), it is one of the prettiest of the festivals, as illuminated paper lanterns of all shapes and sizes are taken to public parks and beaches, notably Victoria Park in Causeway Bay and the main beaches of Lamma, Cheung Chau and Lantau. The Tai Hang Fire Dragon Dance that takes place near Causeway Bay is a highlight. The traditional sweet delicacy known as 'mooncakes', though, are an acquired taste!

41

Film

The entertainment capital of East Asia, Hong Kong has pioneered many genres in the Asian movie industry, from kung fu and high-energy Jackie Chan-style comedies to lavish period adventures like *Crouching Tiger, Hidden Dragon*. The golden days of Hong Kong cinema are past, but the local studio system did produce actors and-directors who have won world recognition. Today Hong Kong's leaner film industry is more outward looking, in particular to China, where its best talents work regularly. Hong Kong's audience is more cosmopolitan and there are always mini film festivals and screenings to discover.

Hollywood of the East

At its height the Hong Kong studios churned out up to 300 movies a year – today less than 30 are probably made here each year. Talented directors and producers look to the larger audience and for budgets in China and elsewhere.

The Oscar-winning *Crouching Tiger, Hidden Dragon* (a joint production between Hong Kong, mainland China, Taiwan and the US), gave filmgoers an appetite for leaping kung fu period dramas.

The phenomenal success of *Crouching Tiger* also propelled local stars Michelle Yeow and Chow Yun-fat into the movie-star firmament, where they take a seat alongside Jackie Chan and the late Bruce Lee. Director John Woo, meanwhile, is one of the hottest directorial talents in the film world.

Film buffs can find out more about locally set films by picking up the two volumes of the *Hong Kong Movie Odyssey* guide, which take you on a personal journey with Hong Kong Tourism Ambassador Jackie Chan into the Hollywood of the East, including tours of many of the locations where classic Hong Kong pictures were filmed.

Hong Kong in Pictures

Love is a Many-Splendored Thing (1955)
This classic Hollywood tear-jerker is set in the early 1950s during the Korean War, and depicts the colonial charm of East-meets-West, 'exotic' Hong Kong, and the problems of inter-racial romance. The film won three Oscars, and much of the setting still exists. William Holden and Jennifer Jones (Hollywood could not then accept a real Chinese actress) go to The Peak – for shopping, dining and attractions – take a sampan ride from Aberdeen Harbour and visit a floating restaurant for a seafood dinner.
The World of Suzie Wong (1960)
A legendary romance between an American artist (William Holden again) and a beautiful local bar girl (now actually played by a Chinese actress,

Below: the Avenue of the Stars celebrates key figures of the Hong Kong movie industry.

Left: a statue of Bruce Lee on the Avenue of Stars.

policemen. The first falls in love with a drug dealer, and the second, a beat policeman in Lan Kwai Fong, pines for his ex-girlfriend and misses the advances of a waitress (Faye Wong). The second part of the film follows the world's longest escalator, the Central-Mid-Levels Escalator.

In the Mood for Love (2000)

One of the Hong Kong greats, this visually exquisite film is another Wong Kar-wai production. Set in the 1950s and 1960s, it features Hong Kong favourites Maggie Cheung and Tony Leung. A story of unrequited love, the film reignited a passion for the elegant and body-hugging qipao dress. Cheung reportedly went through 46 of them during the making of the film, and wears a different one in every scene. They are available at Chinese department stores and speciality shops and boutiques: head for Li Yuen Street West (Central) and Stanley Market.

The Dark Knight (2008)

Batman hit Hong Kong in style in this Academy Award-

Who's Who?

Stars on the promenade include mainland director Zhang Yimou, celebrated globally as an art-house director for films such as *Raise the Red Lantern*, made *Hero* in the same mould as *Crouching Tiger, Hidden Dragon*. Look out for Hong Kong's funniest actor-director, Stephen Chow (*Shaolin Soccer, Kung Fu Hustle*), and the movies of critically acclaimed director Wong Kar-wai (*Chungking Express, Happy Together, In the Mood for Love, 2046*). Hong Kong stars with a worldwide cult following include Bruce Lee, Jackie Chan, Chow Yun-fat, Jet Li and Maggie Cheung. Lately, no-holds-barred violent thrillers such as actor-director Andy Lau's *Infernal Affairs* have captured local and international acclaim – to the extent of being remade by Martin Scorsese and Brad Pitt, as the Oscar-winning *The Departed* – and another all-action Hong Kong director, John Woo, has made the move to Hollywood himself with *Face/Off* and *Mission: Impossible 2*.

Nancy Kwan). Filmed extensively on location – beginning with the Star Ferry – *Suzie Wong* is set in a still-colonial Hong Kong that was only just beginning to boom at the end of the 1950s, and centres on the exciting nightlife of Wan Chai. The Wan Chai of old has gone, but this is still one of the key districts to head for when night falls.

Chungking Express (1994)

Director Wong Kar-wai creates two parallel love stories that focus on two ordinary

Below: the award-winning *Crouching Tiger, Hidden Dragon*.

Above: American films are always showing too.

winning film – the latest in the superhero's franchise. Christian Bale (aka Batman) leaps from the International Finance Centre during his pursuit of the evil mafia accountant, Lau. This was the same building used five years previously in *Lara Croft Tomb Raider: The Cradle of Life,* when Angelina Jolie's character completed the same feat.

Film Festivals

As well as those listed here, various mini film festivals are also held throughout the year. Check the weekly free *HK* magazine and the *South China Morning Post* for details.

Hong Kong International Film Festival
Tel: 2970 3300;
www.hkiff.org.hk; late Mar–Apr
Every spring Hong Kong holds this major two-week festival, featuring premieres, retrospectives, local and Asian films and worldwide cinema as well. Movies are shown in many venues around the city. The festival is part of the Entertainment Expo Hong Kong, which includes the Hong Kong Film Awards Ceremony, Hong Kong Independent Short Film and Video Awards and other film-related events. It is advisable to book ahead online, as tickets sell out fast.

Le French May
Tel: 2388 0002;
www.frenchmay.com; May
Running throughout May, this festival of French culture usually offers a series of classic or new French movies, as well as concerts, exhibitions and many other events.

Hong Kong Lesbian and Gay Film and Video Festival
Tel: 9759 8199;
www.hklgff.hk; Nov
A growing two-week festival featuring screenings, talks and many other events.

Cinemas

There are dozens of cinemas and multiplexes in Hong Kong, which show a mixture of the latest Hollywood releases, local offerings and big-budget Japanese, South Korean or Thai movies. There are also a handful of art-house theatres with European and Asian productions. Almost all non-English films are shown with English subtitles. To find out what is on at any time, check the local English-language press, and especially *HK* magazine and *Time Out Hong Kong*, or their websites.

Evening shows tend to sell out quickly, so it is best to buy in advance. Tickets cost around HK$70, but discounts of around HK$20–30 are offered on tickets all day Tuesday and for morning and matinée shows. Air conditioning in Hong Kong's cinemas can be fierce and many also have booster seats available for children.

AMC
Tel: 2265 8933;
www.amccinemas.com.hk
Operates two plush multiplexes, the **AMC Pacific Place** (MTR: Admiralty) and **AMC Festival Walk** (MTR: Kowloon Tong).

Broadway Circuit
Tel: 2388 0002;
www3.cinema.com.hk
The 11 Broadway movie theatres include **Palace IFC**, in the IFC Mall in Central (MTR: Central/Hong Kong Airport Express

Above: adverts for the annual French film festival.

For art-house movies, try this cinema within the Hong Kong Arts Centre, which regularly shows new and classic films and hosts a variety of film-related events.

Hong Kong Film Archive
50 Lei King Road, Sai Wan Ho;
tel: 2739 2139;
www.filmarchive.gov.hk;
MTR: Sai Wan Ho
Whether you are a film buff or just enjoy Hong Kong movies, do not miss this centre in Sai Wan Ho on the east side of Hong Kong Island. Dedicated to the preservation of Hong Kong's rich film heritage, it offers a fascinating insight into how the industry has developed. There is also a 125-seater cinema, with four wheelchair spaces.

station; map p.137 D4), the city's most luxurious cinema, with big comfy armchair seats. Tickets are standard price; it shows art-house movies as well as mainstream films, has a DVD store and café.

Standing out among other Broadway theatres are the **Cinematheque**, 3 Public Square Street, Yau Ma Tei, Kowloon (MTR: Yau Ma Tei; map p.132 B1), which shows art-house movies and has a small DVD shop and café.

Golden Harvest
www.goldenharvest.com
A major force in local film production, the Golden Harvest company operates the popular **Golden Gateway** (G/F, The Gateway, 25 Canton Road, Tsim Sha Tsui, Kowloon; tel: 2622 6688; MTR: Jordan; map p.134 B2), which shows both first-run English-language and Chinese films.

MCL Cinemas
Tel: 2418 8841;
www.mclcinema.com
Operates three large multiplexes, the **JP Plaza**, Causeway Bay, the **MCL Kornhill** in Quarry Bay, on Hong Kong Island, and the **MCL Cinema Metro** in Tseung Kwan O (MTR: Po Lam).

UA Cinemas
Tel: 2314 4228;
www.cityline.com.hk
UA operates 11 multi-screen movie theatres across Hong Kong Island, Kowloon and the New Territories and iMax screens.

Key cinemas include the **UA Times Square** and **UA Windsor**, both in Causeway Bay (MTR: Causeway Bay), the **iMax@UAiSquare** on Nathan Road (MTR: TST) and the **UA Langham Place**, Argyle Street, Mong Kok, Kowloon (MTR: Mong Kok).

Art-House Cinema

The Broadway Cinematheque in Yau Ma Tei (see above) also shows interesting non-mainstream fare.

Agnès b CINEMA!
Hong Kong Arts Centre, 2 Harbour Road, Wan Chai; tel: 2582 0200; www.hkac.org.hk; MTR: Wan Chai (exit C); map p.138 A3

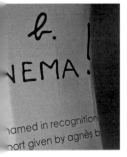

...amed in recognition ...ort given by agnès b

Left: agnès b is the city's leading art-house cinema.

In 2004 Hong Kong made public its affection for its own movie industry with the inauguration of the **Avenue of Stars** along Tsim Sha Tsui harbourside promenade in Kowloon. With an obvious tip of the hat to Hollywood Boulevard, the Avenue captures some of the magic of Hong Kong movies with commemorative plaques (some with handprints of local stars), milestones in Hong Kong's 100-year history of filmmaking, Film Awards sculptures and kiosks selling movie memorabilia. In November 2005, Hong Kong also paid a long-overdue tribute to one of its finest actors when it unveiled a 2m (6ft) high statue of Bruce Lee on the Avenue, on what would have been his 65th birthday. For events on the Avenue, check www.avenueofstars. com.hk. It is worth coming here for the panoramic harbour views alone, and the Avenue is an ideal perch from which to enjoy the Symphony of Lights display at 8pm nightly.

Food and Drink

The Cantonese live to eat, and even as a visitor it is impossible to ignore the major role that food and everything around it plays in the lives of the city. The budget-conscious can feast for next to nothing at home-grown Chinese fast food chains, or for just a few dollars more on seafood or noodles at a seaside restaurant on one of the outer islands; those on a more elastic budget will find thousands of restaurants, countless cuisines and gourmet dining options to choose from. In Hong Kong one thing is for certain: you are never far from good, enjoyable, enticing food.

Cantonese Cuisine

THE BASICS

In the Cantonese system of food preparation, food is cooked quickly and lightly, usually stir-fried in shallow water or an oil base in a wok. Flavours are thus preserved, and not cooked away. Many dishes, particularly vegetables or fish, are steamed. This discourages overcooking, and preserves an ingredient's delicate, natural flavours. Sauces are used to enhance flavours rather than overwhelm them, and the sauce usually contains contrasting ingredients such as vinegar, sugar or ginger.

Communal Dining

The traditional Chinese concept of a meal is very much a communal affair, and one that provides strong sensory impact. Dishes are chosen with both taste and texture in mind, a stomach-pleasing succession of sweet-sour, sharp-bland, hot-cool and crunchy-smooth. If you are invited to join a group of Chinese people for lunch or dinner or a celebratory ban-

Above: dragon fruits.

quet, consider it an honour. Set aside a considerable amount of time for the occasion, and do not eat anything for a while beforehand. A typical meal starts with a cold dish, followed by several main courses. Soup – usually clear, light broth – may be eaten after the heavier courses to aid digestion. If this is a real Chinese banquet, there will be many courses.

Freshness

For an insight into the Chinese passion for the freshest

of food try and visit one of Hong Kong's 'wet' or fresh food markets', selling fruit and vegetables, fish, seafood and meat, so-called wet because floors and stalls are hosed down constantly.

Not unlike Europe, cooks do not start with a particular

Left: live crab for sale, adventurous buyers only.

in doubt opt for lemon chicken, which is completely boned before cooking and served in a lemon sauce flavoured with onions, ginger and sugar. Cantonese barbecuing methods are unrivalled. Try goose, Peking duck or tender slices of pork, with a golden, honeyed skin and served on a bed of anise-flavoured preserved beans.

Dim Sum

A favourite with visitors, and one of Hong Kong's traditional delicacies, dim sum literally translates as 'touch the heart', while yum cha means 'drink tea'. Dim sum snacks – always accompanied by pots of hot tea – were originally served for breakfast, but today are more likely to be eaten around brunch-time.

They take the form of small savoury appetisers, such as *ha gau* (shrimp dumpling), *siu mai* (pork dumpling), *cha siu bau* (barbecued pork bun), *chun gun* (spring roll) and *dun tat* (sweet egg tart). In traditional dim sum restaurants, diners pick from trolleys pushed around by waiters.

dish in mind, but let what is most fresh or in season at the market guide the meal they create. Many have moved indoors now, but even if you are not buying, it is worth popping inside if you spot a sign, or head to the outdoor wet market near Spring Garden Lane, Wan Chai *(see p.102)* or Gage Street in Central to see for yourself just how seriously the Chinese take their food. For anyone who loves food and cooking, this will be a highlight of any visit.

Fish

Fish and seafood are staples in Cantonese cuisine, and best savoured beside the water on Lamma and Cheung Chau, and in Aberdeen and Sai Kung. At many of these restaurants diners get to select a fish or crustacean from huge tanks.

Fish is typically steamed whole with fresh ginger and spring onions, and sprinkled with a little soy sauce and sesame oil. But beware: check the day's 'market price' when you order.

Prawns and crabs – steamed or in a black-bean sauce – are also popular Cantonese dishes.

Meat

Chicken is commonplace, and a single bird is often used to prepare several dishes. Chicken blood is cooked and solidified for soup, and livers are skewered between pieces of pork fat and red-roasted until the fat becomes crisp and the liver soft and succulent. Cantonese chicken dishes can be awkwardly bony for chopsticks beginners, so if

Below: fresh greens.

Above: dim sum.

Each plate taken is marked on a card, and later tallied. But, in many restaurants, menus have replaced the trolleys.

Dim sum is one of the most convivial, most informal and sometimes noisiest ways of eating in Hong Kong, as diners talk loudly across tables and chat back and forth with the trolley-pushing waiters. In a traditional dim sum restaurant, there is no embarrassment at all in pointing to dishes on the trolley, asking what something is, and if you do not understand the answer just trying it out. Go in a group, so you can share and try as many of the little dishes as possible.

Oddities

To many outsiders, some Chinese foods seem bizarre, if not downright repulsive. The famous 'thousand-year eggs' are duck eggs buried in lime for 60 days, with a resulting cheese-like taste.

The search for rare delicacies is common to all Chinese, but the Cantonese have taken it to the extreme. Monkey's brain, bear's paw, snake, dog, pigeon, frog, sparrow, shark's fin, bird's nest and lizard are all sought-after delicacies. Many of the rarest are now either illegal or virtually impossible to obtain in Hong Kong, but do not be surprised to see dried shark's fin piled up in the produce shops of Sheung Wan, snake soup on the menu at a five-star hotel or hundreds of baby frogs or 'field chickens' squirming in a tub at the wet market. Here, they are sold live in plastic bags, and chefs serve them in a crunchy batter mixed with crushed almonds, accompanied by a sweet-and-sour sauce.

Drinks

TEA AND COFFEE

The perfect accompaniment to Chinese food is Chinese tea, which is claimed to have digestive properties and helps counteract some of the

greasiness in Cantonese food. The Chinese have been drinking tea for centuries as a general reviver and ceremonial beverage. Tea in China is drunk without sugar or milk, although 'English tea' or 'milk tea' is widely available if requested. In Hong Kong-style cafés (cha chaan tengs, see p.31) tea is usually served super strong with evaporated or condensed milk.

It is worth making the effort to learn to appreciate the many varieties of Chinese tea and their histories. Strong black teas are popular, but for a caffeine-free alternative,

Below: live squid, live frogs and thousand-year eggs.

Above: Temple Street Night Market.

ask for hot chrysanthemum tea, brewed from the dried petals of the flower.

Tea may have traditionally been first choice in China, but younger Hong Kongers in particular have picked up the international taste for coffee in a big way. Some well-known global coffeehouse chains have firmly planted their brand in Hong Kong and China, but an excellent local alternative is the Pacific Coffee Company, with branches all around Hong Kong, and which also offers free internet access.

WINES AND BEERS

Few visitors develop a taste for Chinese rice wines, despite their 4,000-year history. While some are too sweet, others are too strong. The wheat-based wines are notorious for their alcoholic power. *Mao Tai* is a breathtaking case in point.

The Chinese are not big drinkers – they have a low tolerance level when it comes to alcohol generally – however Hong Kongers are the biggest wine drinkers in Asia. Since the abolition of tax on wine, Hong Kong has become a wine hub attract-

ing auctions and wine appreciation is taken seriously. Red wine, especially French reds are the most popular, and where once XO Cognac was used to impress or seal a business deal, Bordeaux is now the status symbol on the table. Wine appreciation classes and wine pairing dinners are all very popular activities and with eyes firmly upon the growing wine market in China, Hong Kong is now the biannual location for the largest wine fair in the world – Vinexpo.

Every convenience store and supermarket sells a mix of imported beers such as Heineken, Carlsberg, Asahi, Corona, and Hong Kong's locally-brewed best-seller beer. The locally brewed San Miguel is cheap and passable, and Tsing Tao beer from China has a hearty, European taste. You will also find a selection of European brands, real ales and locally-produced microbrews.

Food Blogs

Gadget-loving Hong Kongers combine their love of eating, with photo-taking and discussing food in thousands of food blogs. It's not unusual for a table full of people to pause, pull out SLR cameras and smartphones to photo-

graph each dish before tucking into even the most humble of meals. Online review sites include openrice.com, which attracts a broad spectrum of reviewers. Respected blogs about food in Hong Kong include e-tingfood.com, jasonbonvivant.com and gregoiremichaud.com.

Below: delicate details in a tea shop.

Gay and Lesbian

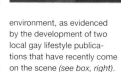

Hong Kong's gay and lesbian community has been getting more prominent over the past few years, as proud pink residents become more vocal about their demands. Nevertheless, many gay and lesbian locals still set up 'marriages of convenience', to show an outward adherence to society values in line with traditional demands to produce family heirs. While this 'fake marriage' practice is lessening, it is still a last resort option for many. Despite progress, gay and lesbian travellers from North America and Western Europe will find acceptance levels here they would never tolerate at home.

Gay Life in Hong Kong

Sexually, young gay and lesbian folk have few options when it comes time to try and find a location for moments of intimacy. This is due to the skyrocketing cost of property and the necessity for most young people to live at home with the family until they marry. As a result, saunas and bathhouses have become incredibly popular getaway spots – especially for young gay men.

The age of consent for men who engage in consensual sex is 16 – the same age as for heterosexuals. This equalisation was only achieved in October 2006, following a challenge by a 20-year-old local in the High Court. Many attribute this change of heart to a more open and accepting local environment, as evidenced by the development of two local gay lifestyle publications that have recently come on the scene *(see box, right)*.

For gay venues, start in Central and Tsim Sha Tsui if you want to party with the local community. Lesbians are at a distinct disadvantage, but there are a few venues in Causeway Bay and TST.

Below: hundreds of people from around the world have come to Hong Kong to protest in favour of gay rights.

Left: only recently has Hong Kong's gay community felt able to protest against discrimination.

A good resource for finding listings and tips is www.utopia.asia.com.

Bars and Clubs

Club 97
9 Lan Kwai Fong, Central; tel: 2810 9333; daily 9pm–1am; MTR: Central; map p.136 C2
While it's only a gay venue on Fridays, Club 97 certainly knows how to pack the bodies in. Pre-dinner Happy Hour runs until 10pm.

New Wally Matt Lounge
Ground Floor, 5A Humphreys Avenue, Tsim Sha Tsui, Kowloon; tel: 2721 2568; www.wallymatt.com; daily 5pm–4am; MTR: Tsim Sha Tsui; map p.134 C2
Popular pub-style after-work drinking spot, with 5–10pm Happy Hours. A great place to meet mostly older HK-resident foreigners.

Propaganda
Lower G/F, 1 Hollywood Road, Central; tel: 2868 1316; Tue–Thur 9pm–4am, Fri–Sat 9pm–5am; free Tue–Thur, entrance charge Fri–Sat; MTR: Central; map p.136 C3
While other gay venues open and close, Propaganda survives and crowds continue to come back due to its legendary status. Things don't get going until at least 1am.

Above: as recently as 2006, the government still promoted conversion therapy to 'cure' gays and lesbians.

Virus
6th Floor, Pak Tak Centre, 268 Jaffe Road, Causeway Bay; tel: 2904 7207; Mon–Sat 9pm–4am; MTR: Causeway Bay; map p.138 B3
This fun karaoke bar is one of the few lesbian-aimed venues in town; gay male friends are also welcome. It's a good place to pick up information on other events around town.

Volume BEAT
G/F 62 Jervois Street, Sheung Wan; tel: 2857 7683; daily 10pm–2.30am; MTR: Sheung Wan; map p.136 B2
The latest addition to the Volume stable of venues celebrating the LGBT lifestyle. BEAT is all about fresh, fun dance music with the occasional drag show.

Volume H.E.A.T
Lower G/F, 83–85 Hollywood Road, Central; tel: 2857 7683; daily noon–midnight; MTR: Central/Sheung Wan; map p.136 B3
Laid-back casual café and tapas bar for daytime lounging with lots of health-conscious dishes. H.E.A.T is big for brunch and is a dining destination in its own right.

Zoo Bar
G/F, 33 Jervois Street, Sheung Wan, tel: 3583 1200; Sun–Fri 6.30pm–2.30am, Sat 7pm–3.30am; MTR: Sheung Wan; map p.136 B2
After dark venue with colourful cocktails, Starting Sunday and Monday with jazz nights, it picks up the pace with packed-out party nights at the weekend.

SEE ALSO NIGHTLIFE, P.76–9

DS (for *Dim Sum*) magazine is the essential guide to gay life in Hong Kong, with listings, features, classifieds and more. It's distributed free through a wide range of outlets, and has a handy website (www.dimsum-hk.com). The same group also produce the monthly *Q Guide*, with a gay map of Hong Kong.

History

C.4000 BC
Aboriginal Yue people set up Stone Age settlements along the coast of South China.

AD 25–220
Han dynasty first extends Chinese imperial rule to the Pearl River area.

969–1279
The Song dynasty. During this time the music and basic styles of Chinese Opera are developed.

12TH CENTURY
The 'Five Clans', Cantonese migrants from further north, settle in the New Territories.

1277–9
Last Song emperor, overthrown by the Mongols, takes refuge in Lantau and near Kowloon.

1577
Portuguese given permission to establish a permanent trading colony at Macau.

1660s
After revolts in South China, the Qing or Manchu dynasty orders the evacuation of many coastal areas. When this is revoked the Hong Kong area is partly resettled by North Chinese migrants called *Hakka*, who form separate communities.

1714
British East India Company establishes trading base in Guangzhou (Canton) to import opium from India. Chinese bans on the trade are ignored.

1839
Commissioner Lin Tse-hsu closes the British Guangzhou factory and confiscates 20,000 chests of opium, sparking the First Opium War.

1841
After China is defeated Britain takes unofficial possession of Hong Kong Island on 26 January, and a year later it is officially ceded to Britain under the Treaty of Nanking. Kowloon is added to the colony in 1860, following the Second Opium War.

1865
Hongkong and Shanghai Bank (HSBC) founded.

1898
New Territories and outlying Islands are leased to Britain for 99 years.

1911
Qing dynasty falls; Sun Yat-sen, educated in Hong Kong, forms the Republic of China.

1937–45
Japan invades China. After they take Guangzhou in 1938, some 750,000 refugees flee to Hong Kong. Japanese troops attack Hong Kong itself on 8 December 1941, and after heavy fighting it falls on Christmas Day. Japanese occupation lasts until 30 August 1945.

1949
Victorious Communists found the People's Republic of China (PRC). The defeated Nationalists flee to Taiwan, and more refugees flood into Hong Kong, where the population swells to 2.2 million.

1966
Pro-Communist riots, inspired by the Cultural Revolution in China, shake Hong Kong.

1979

Mass Transit Railway (MTR) opens.

1984

British Prime Minister Margaret Thatcher and Chinese premier Zhao Ziyang sign 'Joint Declaration' on the future of Hong Kong, agreeing that it will revert to Chinese sovereignty in 1997 as a 'Special Administrative Region' (SAR) of the PRC.

1989

Tiananmen massacre in Beijing leads to large-scale demonstrations in Hong Kong.

1992–7

Chris Patten, the last British governor, seeks to introduce democratic reforms in Hong Kong, including direct elections to the Legislative Council (LegCo).

1997

Handover of sovereignty to China, at midnight on 30 June. Tung Chee-hwa appointed Chief Executive of the SAR, as LegCo is temporarily replaced by a Beijing-appointed Legislature.

1998

New part-elected, part-appointed LegCo established. New airport opens at Chek Lap Kok. Asian economic crisis hits Hong Kong stock market.

2003

Sars kills 299. As Hong Kong's economy stumbles briefly, new measures to encourage tourism from the Mainland launched. Over 500,000 people march against Article 23, a controversial anti-subversion bill, which is shelved.

2005

Tung Chee-hwa resigns and is succeeded by Donald Tsang, a career civil servant under the British. His reform proposals are rejected by democracy campaigners, who say they do not go far enough. Disneyland opens on Lantau.

2006

Hong Kong's Bishop Zen, an outspoken advocate of democracy, becomes a cardinal. In July thousands of Hong Kong people demonstrate for full democracy.

2007

Donald Tsang is re-elected to a new five-year term as Hong Kong's leader, by a committee loyal to Beijing. Hong Kong's 7 million people have no direct say. Nevertheless, the 10th anniversary of the Handover in July is celebrated, as Hong Kong and China's economies boom once again.

2008

Hong Kong hosts equestrian events for the Beijing Olympics. Elections are held for half the seats in LegCo.

2009

Buoyed by China's continued economic growth, Hong Kong emerges from a brief recession.

2011

The gap between Hong Kong's richest and poorest is the widest in Asia. Hong Kong welcomes a record-breaking 40 million visitors.

2012

Hong Kong's third Chief Executive Leung Chun-ying, is elected by the 1,200-person election committee. A turbulent campaign saw pro-establishment voters switch loyalties after a series of scandals discredited their preferred candidate tycoon's son, Henry Tang.

53

Hotels

Hong Kong has some of the most luxurious hotels in the world catering for some of the wealthiest business travellers on the globe. Nearly all the big international hotel groups are represented here. In contrast to the UK and the rest of Europe, hotels in Hong Kong are used as much by the local population as they are by visitors; Hong Kongers frequent hotels for dining, meeting and socialising. The big hotels' afternoon teas and Sunday brunches are renowned, and some of the city's top restaurants and bars are located within the five-star and boutique properties.

Central, the Peak and Western

Bishop Lei International House

4 Robinson Road, Mid-Levels; tel: 2868 0828; www.bishoplei htl.com.hk; $–$$; MTR: Central, then bus to Robinson Road or walk to Mid-Levels Escalator; map p.136 C2

A good low-cost option – owned by the Catholic Diocese of Hong Kong – located 15 minutes' walk away from the nightlife hub of Lan Kwai Fong, and with SoHo on its doorstep (via the Mid-Levels Escalator). There is nothing remarkable about the decor,

but with many of the services and facilities of an upper-scale European hotel – including a gym, business centre, pool, free in-room broadband, 24-hour room service and babysitter and concierge services – this hotel offers value for money. Some suites even have impressive harbour views.

Butterfly on Wellington

122 Wellington Street, Central; tel: 3962 8357; www.butterfly hk.com; $$; MTR: Central; map p.136 C3

Modern, urban hotel with contemporary Asian decor makes for a boutique hotel feel. Part of a small but growing Hong Kong hotel group, like all the Butterfly hotels, Butterfly on Wellington is ideal for guests who want to stay close to the action, and stay connected with free WiFi.

Four Seasons Hong Kong

8 Finance Street, Central; tel: 3196 8888; www.fourseasons. com/hongkong; $$$; MTR: Central, Hong Kong Airport

Left: the indulgent Four Seasons Hong Kong.

The Hong Kong Hotel Association operates meet-and-greet services at exits A and B at the north and south ends of the airport. Reservations are strongly recommended year round, as trade fairs or regional holidays may fill all rooms, but the association also offers reservation services at its counters located beyond the customs hall. If you arrive without a hotel booking, the HKHA will try to help find you a room.

Express; map p.137 C4

With its dazzling facilities (including a large spa and two rooftop pools), hip bars, place-to-be restaurants and jaw-dropping views, the Four Seasons is Hong Kong at its decadent, glamorous, flaunt-it best. If you do not stay, at least try a cocktail in the bar. The hotel has covered access to the Airport Express station and the adjacent chic IFC mall.

Hotel LKF

33 Wyndham Street, Lan Kwai Fong; tel: 3518 9688; www.hotel-lkf.com.hk; $$$; MTR: Central; map p.137 C2

Left: immaculate decor at the hip Hotel LKF.

Price ranges, which are given as a guide only, are for a standard double room with bathroom per night, including service and tax but without breakfast. Note, though, that hotels frequently offer lower promotional rates online, and outside peak seasons.

$	under HK$1,000
$$	HK$1,000–2,000
$$$	over HK$2,000

Not to be confused with the Lan Kwai Fong Hotel *(see p.55)*, the 95-room LKF is one of the city's hippest addresses, smack in the middle of Lan Kwai Fong. Rooms have espresso machines and DVD players, and guests can avail themselves of butler services and complimentary shoeshine. The sexy 29th-floor Azure Restaurant Slash Bar is one of the city's best. Booking in advance is recommended to ensure a table.

Island Shangri-La
Pacific Place, Supreme Court Road, Central; tel: 2877 3838; www.shangri-la.com; $$$; MTR: Admiralty; map p.137 E2
The jaw-dropping 17-storey atrium at 'the Shang' says it all: this is the Shangri-La group's flagship property, and comes with all the bells, whistles and first-class service one would expect from this revered local chain. Large rooms with oversize bathrooms have broadband, DVDs, in-room copier/printers and other gadgets, and views of the harbour or Victoria Peak. The restaurants are heavily patronised by local gourmets – always a good sign.

Lan Kwai Fong Hotel
3 Kau U Fong, Sheung Wan; tel: 3650 0000; www.lankwaifong hotel.com.hk; $$; MTR: Sheung Wan; map p.136 C3
There is a boutique Asian charm to this 162-room hotel, and its location – west of the real Lan Kwai Fong district, not far from Hollywood Road, the Man Mo Temple and SoHo – is excellent. There is in-house dining and internet access, and five suites have balconies (almost unheard of in Hong Kong) with spectacular views across Central to the harbour. The balconies are not for vertigo sufferers, however.

Below: Island Shangri-La.

Above: greeting guests at the Mandarin Oriental.

Mandarin Oriental Hong Kong
5 Connaught Road, Central; tel: 2522 0111; www.mandarin oriental.com; $$$; MTR: Central; map p.137 D3

Mandarin Oriental's first and flagship property reopened at the end of 2006 after a major refit, with larger rooms, multilingual butlers on every floor and iPod docking stations as standard. Service remains exemplary, and the hotel has lost none of its charm to modernity. The Mandarin also houses a clutch of popular restaurants and bars, including the Conran-revamped **Mandarin Grill** and a bar that has a special licence to permit smoking, in spite of Hong Kong's recent smoking ban.
SEE ALSO RESTAURANTS, P.87

Wan Chai and Causeway Bay

Cosmo Hotel
375–377 Queen's Road East, Wan Chai; tel: 3552 8388; www. cosmohotel.com.hk; $; MTR: Causeway Bay; map p.138 C2

The Cosmo, with its imaginative colour-coded orange, green or pastel-yellow rooms and retro wallpaper, is funky and an exceptionally well-priced option. Its location, in a historic building a stone's throw from Happy Valley Racecourse and the Causeway Bay shopping district, makes it perfect for keen shoppers, and Wan Chai's nightlife is also on the doorstep. There's free WiFi access throughout, and the many nice touches for a hotel in this price range include flat-panel PCs with broadband access in the executive rooms.

Empire Hotel
8 Wing Hing Street, Wan Chai; tel: 2866 9111, www.empire hotel.com.hk; $$; MTR: Wan Chai; map p.139 C3

A good-value hotel in the heart of Wan Chai, the 360-room Empire has many of the services and facilities of its higher-priced neighbours, including a pool, gym and business centre. Rooms are pleasantly comfortable, and there is no scrimping on in-room amenities.

Fleming Hong Kong
41 Fleming Road, Wan Chai; tel: 3607 2288; www.thefleming. com.hk; $$; MTR: Wan Chai; map p.138 B3

Dubbing itself Hong Kong's 'Urban Lifestyle Hotel', the Fleming is a new 66-room boutique property in the thick of Wan Chai. WiFi, cordless phones and plasma TVs are standard, and there is free access to a DVD library. Deluxe and executive rooms have kitchenettes. Asia's first female-only floor caters for women guests with in-room beauty kits, jewellery boxes, facial steamers and toiletries.

Grand Hyatt Hong Kong
1 Harbour Road, Wan Chai; tel: 2588 1234; www.hong kong.grand.hyatt.com; $$$; MTR: Wan Chai; map p.138 A3

The Hyatt has magnificent views of the Convention Centre and harbour, and its grand Art Deco-style lobby with black marble pillars, mosaic floor and sweeping staircase is a sight to behold. Hints of Art Deco continue through the public areas and luxuriously minimalist guest rooms. The hotel is also known for its **Plateau Spa** – a state-of-the-art fitness, spa and pool complex that extends over 7,000 sq m (75,000 sq ft). Other facilities include tennis courts, a golf driving range, jogging track and a fabulous Champagne Bar.
SEE ALSO PAMPERING, P.81

J-Plus Boutique Hotel
1–5 Irving Street, Causeway Bay; tel: 3196 9000; www.jia hongkong.com; $$–$$$; MTR: Causeway Bay; map p.139 D3

Price ranges, which are given as a guide only, are for a standard double room with bathroom per night, including service and tax but without breakfast. Note, though, that hotels frequently offer lower promotional rates online, and outside peak seasons.
$ under HK$1,000
$$ HK$1,000–2,000
$$$ over HK$2,000

You will want for nothing at one of Hong Kong's upmarket hotels: excellent city and/or harbour views are pretty much guaranteed, and in low season you should not have to pay any more for a view. Interconnecting rooms are often available for families. Always request a view when booking, and ask about free room upgrades and seasonal packages: many of these include benefits such as food and drinks credits, and free laundry service.

Also, remember that almost all hotels offer free local phone calls, and many of the newer establishments and smaller boutique hotels now offer free WiFi access. To meet ever increasing visitor numbers more land has been allocated for hotel projects. Dozens more hotels will be opening after 2012 in Sheung Wan and Western on Hong Kong Island and Kowloon.

Stylish, urbane and stuffed with objets d'art, J-Plus Boutique Hotel, bears plenty of the quirky hallmarks associated with designer Philippe Starck. The 54 studio-rooms are far from large, but they are certainly stunning, and you will want for nothing in this service-oriented hotel. Complimentary breakfast, afternoon cakes, cocktail-hour wine and gym access make the rates very good value.

Lanson Place
133 Leighton Road, Causeway Bay; tel: 3477 6888; www.lansonplace.com; $$–$$$; MTR: Causeway Bay; map p.139 D3

Opened in mid-2006, the Lanson differentiates itself from Hong Kong's other boutique hotels with its distinctly European accent. Smart, airy and sophisti-

cated, it offers free WiFi and use of the DVD and book library, a complimentary 'wellness' breakfast and gym access. Some rooms have kitchenettes. Sip a martini in their lounge or ask the sommelier to recommend a vintage wine.

Southside
Le Méridien Cyberport
100 Cyberport Road, Pok Fu Lam, near Aberdeen; tel: 2980 7788; www.hongkong.lemeridien.com; $$$; bus: 40 to Pok Fu Lam, or free hotel shuttle bus

Perched on the edge of Telegraph Bay west of Aberdeen, the 173-room Le Méridien Cyberport is one of Hong Kong's most spectacular, 'world of its own' hotels (although Central is only a 15-minute taxi ride away), and one of the city's funkiest to boot. The panoramas from the ocean-view rooms are memorable, and cocktails in its trendy bar are a must at sunset. It is a stone's throw away from Cyberport, a revolutionary digital city that also features a cinema and a plethora of high-end shops, and the hotel's electronic facilities are accordingly state-of-the-art. Nearby attractions include Repulse Bay, South Bay Beach, Stanley Market and Big Wave

Bay. Ocean Park is only minutes away too.

Kowloon
Eaton Smart Hong Kong
380 Nathan Road, Jordan; tel: 2782 1818; http://hongkong.eatonhotels.com; $–$$; MTR: Jordan; map p.134 B4

Eaton Smart provides the service and amenity levels of its parent company the Langham Group at an affordable price. Located a little far north to be perfect, it offers easy access via the nearby MTR station. What you lose in terms of harbour views and convenience, you more than make up for in the form of the money you'll save in your pocket.

Harbour Grand Kowloon
20 Tak Fung Street, Whampoa Gardens, Hung Hom; tel: 2621 3188; www.harbour-plaza.com; $$; MTR: Hung Hom

With its rooftop resort-style pool and impressive waterfront views, the Harbour Plaza, near Whampoa Gardens on the east side of Kowloon, is a popular choice among visiting Chinese leaders. Though it is slightly out on a limb, there are still scores of shops and restaurants on the doorstep, plus a ferry to North Point and free shuttle bus to TST, East TST and Hung Hom MTR stations.

Below: Harbour Grand Kowloon hotel.

It is only a short ferry ride or MTR journey between the two, but make sure you know which side of the harbour you want to be on before booking your accommodation: Kowloon (Tsim Sha Tsui) or Hong Kong Island (where Central, Lan Kwai Fong, Wan Chai and Causeway Bay are the key areas). Kowloon is where most of the markets and tourist shopping is located, but if nightlife is a key criterion then you should opt to stay on Hong Kong Island.

Holiday Inn Golden Mile

50 Nathan Road, Tsim Sha Tsui; tel: 2369 3111; www.golden mile.com; $$; MTR: Tsim Sha Tsui; map p.134 C1

This hotel is conveniently located in the middle of Nathan Road's 'Golden Mile' shopping strip; the modern rooms, in the usual Holiday Inn style, are a good size and feature floor-to-ceiling windows, although any hope of a nice view is blocked by the nearby buildings. It has a varied mix of good restaurants, such as the **Bistro on the Mile**, and there is a rooftop swimming pool and spa available.

SEE ALSO RESTAURANTS, P.94

Intercontinental Hong Kong

18 Salisbury Road, Tsim Sha Tsui; tel: 2721 1211; www.hong kong-ic.intercontinental.com; $$$; MTR: Tsim Sha Tsui; map p.134 C1

One of Hong Kong's top hotels, with possibly the best harbourfront views in town, right on the Tsim Sha Tsui waterfront. The Lobby Bar and rooftop infinity spa pools are not to be missed, and the hotel also boasts Asia's most decadent presidential suite, cantilevered over the harbour (with its own infinity pool and gym). Dining options include the region's first **Nobu** outside Tokyo, as well as **SPOON by Alain Ducasse**. There is also the luxurious **I-Spa**. Rooms are generously sized and well appointed, and most have harbour views.

Below: the Intercontinental Hong Kong has some of the city's finest views.

Opposite: Philippe Starck's boutique design at the J-Plus Boutique Hotel in Causeway Bay *(see p.56)*.

Langham Place Hotel

555 Shanghai Street, Mong Kok; tel: 3552 3388; www.hong kong.langhamplacehotels.com; $$; MTR: Mong Kok; map p.132 B3

This hotel is part of a multi-purpose office, leisure and hotel complex that rises like a shiny new incisor from a formerly rundown patch of Mong Kok. The hi-tech rooms have floor-to-ceiling windows over a fascinatingly vibrant district of Hong Kong, and facilities include guest phones that can be taken anywhere in the hotel (and let you check the world weather, news headlines and your stocks and shares), WiFi throughout, huge in-room plasma screens and DVD. The impressively large **Chuan Spa** is among the city's best hotel spas. A 15-storey entertainment complex, which includes a **UA Cinema**, is next door.

SEE ALSO FILM, P.45; PAMPERING, P.80

Luxe Manor

39 Kimberley Road, Tsim Sha Tsui; tel: 3763 8888; www.the luxemanor.com; $$–$$$; MTR: Tsim Sha Tsui; map p.134 C2

The first boutique designer hotel in Kowloon, Luxe Manor offers a modern, or perhaps postmodern, interpretation of a European mansion. Some of its design features recall the works of 20th-century Surrealists, and the whimsically themed rooms are sure to appeal to anyone with a sense of humour. Each room has a great rain shower, but no bath; free breakfast is served at the hotel's Aspasia restaurant. The Luxe also offers a good location, at the heart of the Tsim Sha Tsui shopping district and just a short walk away from the Knutsford Terrace dining and bar area.

The Mira

118 Nathan Road, TST; tel: 2368 1111; www.themira hotel.com; $$–$$$; MTR: TST; map p.134 C2

Once known as the Miramar, The Mira was reborn as a design-conscious hotel with fresh attitude and is part of the regeneration of the Tsim Sha Tsui area. Enjoying a great location for shopping and exploring. Some rooms enjoy green views towards Kowloon Park. Superb restaurants and spacious spa in basement.

Nathan Hotel

378 Nathan Road, Yau Ma Tei, tel: 2388 5141, www.nathan hotel.com; $$; MTR: Yau Ma Tei; map p.134 B4

This renovated, quiet and pleasant hotel is close to the Temple Street Night Market, and has 180 spacious and well-decorated no-frills rooms. The Penthouse restaurant serves Cantonese and Western food, and there is a Starbucks on site.

Right: Langham Hotel, Tsim Sha Tsui.

Above: Salisbury YMCA.

Novotel Hong Kong Nathan Road Kowloon
348 Nathan Road, Yau Ma Tei; tel: 3965 8888; www.novotel.com; MTR: Jordan; $$; map p.134 C4

This smart hotel offers extremely comfortable accommodation with some neat design touches. Relaxed and stylish, plus live entertainment nightly in a cool hotel bar. Well-located for exploring all parts of the city.

The Peninsula
Salisbury Road, Tsim Sha Tsui; tel: 2920 2888; www.peninsula.com/hongkong; $$$; MTR: Tsim Sha Tsui; map p.134 C1

The much-loved 'Pen' opened in 1928, making it Hong Kong's most historic hotel. Today, one only has to step into the magnificent lobby, where the famous afternoon tea is served, to imbibe the ambience of yesteryear. But the Peninsula also has both feet planted firmly in the present. Rooms are the pinnacle of luxury, matching the hotel's helipad and fleet of Rollers, and the views from the famous corner-suite baths are legendary. In-house establishments include the Philippe Starck-designed **Felix** top-floor bar, with its celebrated men's loo with a view, and the **Peninsula Spa by ESPA**.

SEE ALSO PAMPERING, P.81; RESTAURANTS, P.95

Salisbury YMCA
41 Salisbury Road, Tsim Sha Tsui; tel: 2369 2211; www.ymca hk.org.hk; $$; MTR: Tsim Sha Tsui; map p.134 B1

Its room rates do not follow those found in your typical YMCA, but the Salisbury is nonetheless one of the best bargains in the city, offering the facilities and service of much more expensive hotels at a fraction of the cost. Rooms are utilitarian but comfortable and well equipped, and there is a pool, gym, squash courts, climbing wall and on-site dining. Try and splurge on one of the harbour-view rooms, where you can enjoy the vistas that nearby Peninsula guests savour.

W Hong Kong
1 Austin Road West, Kowloon Station; tel: 3717 2222; www.w-hongkong.com; $$$; MTR: Kowloon; map p.134 A3

Kowloon's latest addition was this branch of the design hotel chain, W. Opened in late 2008, it has put the emerging neighbourhood of West Kowloon on the map. The usual chic and cheerful interiors for which the W group is known apply. Additional touches include a rooftop swimming pool, popular **Living Room** bar

Below: sleek style at the W Hong Kong's reception.

Above: The Peninsula, Hong Kong Tsim Sha Tsui, Kowloon.

Hong Kong's hotel rates can boom steep, especially when 10 percent service charge is added to the bill. But standards are among the best in the world, and you can be assured of modern and tasteful rooms, first-rate facilities, spotless public areas, 24-hour room service, a staggering choice of bars and dining options and exceptional service. Many hotels also have shopping malls on site. And there are ways of cutting down on the cost of staying in Hong Kong, above all by booking online or through a tour operator that deals extensively in the region: hotels are continually offering special rates on their websites, which are often far lower than their theoretical standard rates.

and the signature Whatever-Whenever concierge service.
SEE ALSO BARS AND CAFÉS, P.31

New Territories
Hyatt Regency Hong Kong, Sha Tin
18 Chak Cheung Street, Sha Tin; tel: 3723 1234; www.hong kong.shatin.hyatt.com; $$–$$$; MTR: University

2009 brought the New Territories its first-ever property from an international hotel group. Like most Hyatt hotels, it is suitably grand yet firmly focuses its attentions on the needs of its core business traveller. Expect comfortable rooms lacking a little in terms of charm – but great value, especially if compared to similar hotels in Kowloon or on the island.

Royal Park
8 Pak Hok Ting Street, Sha Tin, tel: 2601 2111, www.royal park.com.hk; $$; MTR: East line to Sha Tin

This recently refurbished and

surprisingly stylish hotel near Sha Tin's New Town Plaza shopping complex and over-looking the Shin Mun River is easily accessed from the city by KCR, or on the hotel's own shuttle buses to and from Tsim Sha Tsui. There are three Asian restaurants, a coffee shop, squash and tennis courts, jogging facilities and a swimming pool and health centre. Special facilities are also provided for guests with disabilities.

The Outer Islands
Hong Kong Disneyland Hotel and Disney's Hollywood Hotel
Hong Kong Disneyland Resort, Lantau; tel: 3510 6000, 3510 5000; www.hongkongdisney land.com; $$$; MTR: Sunny Bay, then change to Disneyland Resort Line

If visiting Hong Kong with younger children, you might find it hard to miss out on spending at least one night here. Both hotels are 10

Price ranges, which are given as a guide only, are for a standard double room with bathroom per night, including service and tax but without breakfast. Note, though, that hotels frequently offer lower promotional rates online, and outside peak seasons.
$ under HK$1,000
$$ HK$1,000–2,000
$$$ over HK$2,000

mins from the airport and 25 mins from downtown, and there are complimentary shuttle buses between the hotels and Disneyland itself. The former hotel is Victorian style, the latter all-American. A variety of packages are available, combining hotel accommodation with park entrance.

Hong Kong Sky City Marriott
1 Sky City Road East, Hong Kong International Airport, Lantau; tel: 3969 1888; www.marriott.com; $$; MTR: AsiaWorld-Expo

One of two airport hotels to choose from, the Sky City Marriott is especially convenient for anyone travelling to shows at the nearby Asia-World Expo or anyone needing a convenient place to rest their head while in transit. Free shuttles keep it within easy reach of the airport whatever the time of day.

Warwick Hotel
East Bay, Cheung Chau; tel: 2981 0081; www.warwickhotel. com.hk; $–$$; Ferry: Cheung Chau

This island-resort beach hotel houses 70 rooms, albeit in an ugly grey concrete building. All rooms have balconies with views straight onto a fine beach, and facilities include a children's playground, babysitting services, a pool and facilities for watersports.

61

Language

Hong Kong's official languages are Chinese and English. The main Chinese dialect is Cantonese, spoken by more than 90 percent of the population and an inseparable part of the sound and rhythm of the city. Mandarin Chinese (Putonghua), the official language of the People's Republic of China, is gaining in popularity. This reflects the importance of doing business with the mainland and inbound tourism rather than government directives. Cantonese can seem rather daunting to speakers of European languages, but an attempt at a simple phrase or two will generally be well received.

A Language Minefield

Hong Kong people use a standard form of Cantonese when they write, or in a business situation, but speak colloquial Cantonese in everyday conversation. Colloquial Chinese is rich in slang, and some spoken words do not have characters.

To confuse you further, Hong Kong (like Taiwan) uses a slightly different style of characters to the rest of China. During reforms initiated by Mao in the 1950s to increase literacy, the People's Republic of China simplified its characters. Hence the characters used on the mainland are referred to as Simplified Chinese, while Hong Kong's more complex characters are called Traditional Chinese.

> The written form of Chinese was originally derived from pictures or symbols that represented objects or concepts, so there is no correlation between the appearance of Chinese characters and the sound that they represent.

TONES

If all this was not enough to master, many an enthusiastic linguist has been defeated by Cantonese tones. Each word has a distinct pitch that goes higher, lower or stays flat within each word. Among the Cantonese there is no real agreement as to how many tones there are – some say as many as nine – but most people use six in daily life.

The Jyutping transliteration system devised by the Linguistic Society of Hong Kong classifies the six main tones as: **1**, high falling/high flat; **2**, high rising; **3**, middle; **4**, low falling; **5**, low rising; **6**, low.

Each word has one syllable, and is represented by one distinct character. A word is made up of three sound elements: an initial, e.g. 'f', plus a final sound, e.g. 'an', plus a tone.

A few rare words just have a final sound and a tone, e.g. 'm' in *m goi* (thank you).

Therefore, when combined with a tone, 'fan' has seven distinct and contradictory meanings: flour (high falling 1); to divide (high rising 2); to teach (middle flat 3); fragrant (high flat 1); a grave (low falling 4); energetic (low rising 5); and a share (low flat 6).

The wealth of sound-alike words (homonyms) that can easily be mispronounced play a part in many Cantonese traditions and the development of slang. However, for the visitor or new learner tones mean that utter bafflement is a common reaction to your attempt simply to say the name of the road you wish to visit. Persevere, and try to mimic the way a Cantonese speaker says each part of the phrase.

Pronunciation

j as in the 'y' of yap
z similar to the sound in be**ig**e or the zh in Guang**zh**ou
c as in chip
au as in how
ai as in buy
ou as in no
i as in he

Useful Words and Phrases

NUMBERS

0	*ling*
1	*jat*

Left: the written word can be a delicate art.

PEOPLE
mother *maa maa*
father *baa baa*
son *zai*
daughter *neoi*
baby *be be*
friend *pang jau*
boyfriend *naam pang jau*
girlfriend *neoi pang jau*
husband *lou gung*
wife *lou po*

ADJECTIVES
small *sai*
big *daaih*
good *ho*
bad *waaih*
expensive *gwai*
cheap *pehng*
slow *maan*
fast *faai*
pretty/beautiful *leng*
hot *jit*
cold *dung*
very… *hou …*
delicious *ho sick*

HEALTH AND EMERGENCIES
I have (a) … *ngo…*
headache *tau tung*
stomach ache *tou tung*
toothache *nga tung*
fever *faat sui*
I am sick *ngo jau beng*
doctor *ji sang*
nurse *wu si*
ambulance *gau surng che*
police *ging chaat*

2	*ji*
3	*saam*
4	*sei*
5	*ng*
6	*luk*
7	*cat*
8	*baat*
9	*gau*
10	*sap*
11	*sap jat*
12	*sap ji*
20	*ji sap*
21	*ji sap jat*
100	*baak*
140	*jat sei ling*

COMMON EXPRESSIONS
Good morning *jo sahn*
Good afternoon *ng on*
Good night *zou tau*
Goodbye *jo geen*
Hello (on phone) *wai!*
Thank you (service) *m goi*
Thank you (gift) *daw jeh*
You're welcome *msai*
No problem *mou man tai*
How are you? *Nei hou maa?*
(neigh ho marr)
Fine, thank you *gay ho, yau sum*
yes *haih*
no *mhai*
OK *hou aa*
Please take me to *m goy chey ngor hur-ee*

My name is… *ngor geeu*
yesterday *kum yut*
today *gum yut*
tomorrow *ting yut*
hotel *zau dim*
key *so si*
manager *ging lei*
room *haak fong*
telephone *din wa*
toilet *ci so*
bank *ngan hong*
post office *yau jing guk*
passport *wu ziu*
restaurant *zaan teng*
bar *zau ba*
bus *ba si*
taxi *dik si*
train *fo ze*

QUESTIONS
Who? *bin go a?*
Where? *bin do a?*
When? *gei si a?*
Why? *dim gaai a?*
How many? *gei do a?*
How much does that cost? *gay daw?*
Do you have…? *yau mo … a?*
What time is the train to Guangzhou…? *Guangzhou ge for che, gay dim hoy a?*

Right: a calligrapher's shop.

Museums and Galleries

Hong Kong's museums and galleries have an enviable task: to document the thriving, modern culture of Hong Kong set against rich Chinese traditions, and all the while preserve a unique colonial past. This puts the city's heritage at the visitor's fingertips, whether in the delicacy of tea ware at Flagstaff House or the sweeping political changes recorded at the Hong Kong Heritage Museum. There is also a vibrant art scene, revealed at the Hong Kong Museum of Art and Arts Centre.

Art Museum of The Chinese University of Hong Kong

Ma Liu Shui, near Sha Tin, New Territories; tel: 3943 7416; www.cuhk.edu.hk/ics/amm; daily 10am–5pm; free; MTR: East line to University station, then shuttle bus

The Chinese University campus enjoys a panoramic view over the scenic inland waters of Tolo Harbour. The purpose-built Art Museum showcases Chinese art to brilliant effect and, in association with mainland Chinese museums, has brought many Chinese treasures to Hong Kong in exciting temporary exhibitions. The permanent collection includes paintings, calligraphy, bronze seals and jade carvings.

Asia Society Hong Kong Center

The Hong Kong Jockey Club Former Explosives Magazine, 9 Justice Drive, Admiralty; tel: 2103 9511; www.asiasociety.org/hongkong; Tue–Sun 11am–5pm; admission; MTR Admiralty exit C1; bus/tram: Queensway; map p.137 D2

Opened in 2012, this dynamic new gallery combines new constructions with 19th century buildings that once stored explosives. The Asia Society Hong Kong Center's galleries and theatre present regular exhibitions and public lectures. There's a café, museum shop and roof garden too. For history and military buffs the centre runs regular heritage tours as well as its docent-led tours of exhibitions.

Flagstaff House Museum of Tea Ware

10 Cotton Tree Drive, Hong Kong Park, Central; tel: 2869 0690, www.lcsd.gov.hk; daily 10am–5pm; free; MTR: Admiralty, bus/tram: Queensway; map p.137 D2

The building housing this museum, the oldest surviving colonial building in Hong Kong, is every bit as interesting (or more so) as the exhibit itself. Flagstaff House was completed in 1846, and for over a century was the residence of the Commander-in-Chief of the British Army in Hong Kong, as the centre of the area known as Victoria Barracks. Today, the large expanse is the lush, green Hong Kong Park, which is also the site of a popular aviary. The

Below: Museum of Tea Ware.

Left: Hong Kong Arts Centre (see p.68).

www.hkmaritimemuseum.org; Tue–Sun 10am–6pm; entrance charge; MTR Hong Kong, Central; map p.137 D4
Open in 2013, the maritime museum moved to this magnificent new location at Pier 8 from Stanley. Galleries are devoted to seafaring Hong Kong, China trade, piracy, underwater archaeology and real-time information on everything that is happening in the harbour today.

Hong Kong Museum of Art

Hong Kong Cultural Centre, 10 Salisbury Road, Tsim Sha Tsui, Kowloon; tel: 2721 0116; www.lcsd.gov.hk/hkma; Fri and Sun–Wed 10am–6pm, Sat 10am–8pm; entrance charge, but free Wed; MTR: Tsim Sha Tsui; map p.134 C1
The box-shaped Museum of Art on the Kowloon waterfront is a great place to while away a few hours. The museum houses some of the world's finest examples of ancient Chinese art, from the Han to the Ming and Qing dynasties, along with hundreds of traditional and contemporary oil paintings,

Below: Hong Kong Museum of Arts.

museum hosts a very extensive display of historic pots, cups and the many different artefacts associated with tea in China, as well as temporary exhibits on various aspects of Chinese tea and tea-drinking, and occasionally of modern potters' tea ware.

Hong Kong Correctional Services Museum

45 Tung Tau Wan Road, Stanley, Southside; tel: 2147 3199; www.csd.gov.hk/english/hkcsm/hkcsm.html; Tue–Sun 10am–5pm; free; bus: 6, 6X, 40, 66, 260
A Hong Kong oddity: in the peaceful setting of Stanley, this museum charts the history of the Hong Kong penal system from the early days of the colony, with creepy exhibits like a mock gallows and cells.

Some of Hong Kong's attractions are especially suited to little travellers. For more information on child-friendly places to visit, *see p.32–3.*

Hong Kong Heritage Museum

1 Man Lam Road, Sha Tin, New Territories; tel: 2180 8188; www.heritagemuseum.gov.hk; Mon and Wed–Sat 10am–6pm, Sun 10am–7pm; entrance charge; MTR: Che Kung, 80M; bus from Kowloon Tong MTR
Designed to preserve and interpret the cultural identity of Hong Kong, this is also the territory's largest museum, with 12 exhibition halls in an all-new building designed to evoke traditional Chinese architecture through a series of attractive courtyards.

In addition to hosting changing thematic exhibitions, the permanent galleries include an exquisite gallery of Chinese art and exhibits devoted to the development of the New Territories and their varied ethnic groups, the history of Cantonese opera and even the evolution of local toys. Displays are comprehensive and imaginative.

Hong Kong Maritime Museum

Pier 8, Central Ferry Pier, Central tel: 2813 2322;

Above: Hong Kong Museum of Art.

drawings, etchings and calligraphy. It also displays historic photographs, prints and artefacts from Hong Kong, Macau and Guangzhou. Four of the seven exhibition galleries are taken up with Chinese antiquities, Chinese fine arts, historical pictures and contemporary local art. Worldwide collections are also showcased, in two special exhibition galleries.

Hong Kong Museum of Coastal Defence

175 Tung Hei Road, Shau Kei Wan, east of Causeway Bay; tel: 2569 1500; www.lcsd.gov.hk; Fri–Wed 10am–5pm; entrance charge, but free Wed; MTR: Shau Kei Wan or Heng Fa Chuen Located in the restored 19th-century Lei Yue Mun Fort, this museum documents Hong Kong's military past, from the Ming and Qing dynasties to colonial times, World War II and the present day. The permanent exhibition is located in the 1887 Redoubt, which is the starting point for a historical trail where visitors can view restored military installations, including a World War II tank.

Hong Kong Museum of History

100 Chatham Road South, Tsim Sha Tsui East, Kowloon; tel:

2724 9042; www.hk.history. museum; Mon and Wed–Sat 10am–6pm, Sun 10am–7pm; entrance charge, but free Wed; MTR: TST, East TST; bus: Chatham Road South; map p.135 D3 Conveniently opposite the Science Museum (see opposite) this large and lavish modern showcase museum documents 6,000 years of Hong Kong history, from its earliest settlement to the Chinese dynasties, the colonial era and the 1997 Handover through its permanent exhibition The Hong Kong Story. Imaginative, lively and sometimes perhaps surprisingly controversial displays include lifelike mock-ups of old-style teahouses, cinemas and a Cantonese opera stage.

Hong Kong Museum of Medical Sciences

2 Caine Lane, Western; tel: 2549 5123; www.hkmms.org.hk; Tue–Sat 10am–5pm, Sun 1–5pm; entrance charge; MTR: Central, then Mid-Levels Escalator; bus: Caine Road; map p.136 B3 Housed in a historic monument – a distinguished Edwardian building from 1906 that was Hong Kong's first purpose-built medical laboratory – this museum is one of the first in the world to compare the traditional Chinese and Western

approaches to medicine. The old Bacteriological Institute laboratory is still intact.

Hong Kong Racing Museum

2/F Happy Valley Stand, Happy Valley; tel: 2966 8065; www.hkjc.com; Tue–Sun 10am–5pm; free; bus/tram: Happy Valley; map p.138 C1 Horse racing began in Hong Kong at the justifiably famous Happy Valley Racecourse in 1845, but if you cannot make it to the actual races, visit this colourful museum, opened in 1996. The museum's glass wall looks over the high-tech racecourse and stands, and it tells the history of racing in the former colony via eight galleries, a cinema and interactive videos.
SEE ALSO SPORT, P.112

Hong Kong Railway Museum

13 Shung Tak Street, Tai Po Market, Tai Po, New Territories; tel: 2653 3455; www.heritage museum.gov.hk; Wed–Mon 9am–5pm; free; KCR: East line

Hong Kong is a famously safe city for visitors, with street and petty crime a rare occurrence. But for a glimpse into Hong Kong's underworld, and the infamous Triads, be sure to pop into the **Police Museum**, in the former Wan Chai Gap police station. It traces the history of the former Royal Hong Kong Police Force, which today has dropped the 'Royal', through four sections: an orientation gallery, a gallery for temporary exhibitions and, most gripping, the Triad Societies and Narcotics Galleries. 27 Coombe Road, The Peak; tel: 2849 7019; Tue 2–5pm, Wed–Sun 9am–5pm; free; bus: 15 from Central.

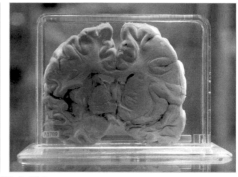

Above: Hong Kong Museum of Medical Sciences.

to Tai Po Market, bus: 271 from Canton Road, Kowloon

This small, picturesque museum is a must-see for railway enthusiasts, but its historical charm and quaintness will also appeal across the board. It is located in the Chinese-temple-style former Tai Po Market railway station on the Guangzhou line, which first opened in 1913, and is now a historic monument. The museum charts the development both of the Kowloon-Canton Railway and of the town of Tai Po – one of the oldest in the New Territories – and exhibits include atmospheric photographs and a full-size model of an electric train compartment, as well as real steam locomotives and vintage coaches.

Hong Kong Science Museum

2 Science Museum Road, Tsim Sha Tsui East, Kowloon; tel: 2732 3232; http://hk.science. museum; Mon–Wed and Fri 1–9pm, Sat–Sun 10am–9pm; entrance charge, but free Wed; MTR: TST, East TST; bus: Chatham Road South; map p.135 D3

Unreservedly directed at the young, whether in families or school groups, the Science Museum displays more than 500 scientific and technological interactive exhibits, including robotics, computers, phones, a miniature submarine, a DC–3 aeroplane and a 22m (72ft) high Energy Machine which, when activated, triggers a series of spectacular audio-visual displays. With 80 percent of its exhibits hands-on, this is a great place for kids to explore the basic concepts of science and technology. It is enormously popular, but adults without kids in tow might find it less interesting.

Hong Kong Space Museum

Salisbury Road, Tsim Sha Tsui, Kowloon; tel: 2721 0226; www.lcsd.gov.hk; Mon and Wed–Fri 1–9pm, Sat–Sun 10am–9pm; entrance charge, but main exhibition free Wed; MTR: Tsim Sha Tsui; map p.134 C1

The igloo-like Space Museum with its trademark domed roof abuts the Hong Kong Museum of Art on the Kowloon waterfront. There are two exhibition halls – the Hall of Space Science and Hall of Astronomy – with the emphasis, as in the Science Museum, on interactive exhibits, with plenty to keep kids fascinated. There is also the giant Space Theatre planetarium (extra charge), which presents two types of show: the Sky Show, on a 23m (75ft) dome screen, and documentaries on a 360-degree Omnimax screen.

Below: Hong Kong Science Museum.

Above: Chinese painting, past and present.

Hong Kong Visual Arts Centre

Hong Kong Park, 7A Kennedy Road, Central; tel: 2521 3008; www.lcsd.gov.hk; Wed–Mon 10am–9pm; free; MTR: Admiralty, bus/tram: Queensway, Cotton Tree Drive; map p.137 D2

Housed in the officers' quarters of the former Victoria Barracks, this centre is a strong supporter of local art and artists, specialising in the fields of sculpture, printmaking and pottery. It comprises nine well-equipped working studios, an exhibition space and a lecture theatre, and hosts a varied mix of events, workshops, exhibitions

demonstrations and artist-in-residence programmes.

Pao Galleries, Hong Kong Arts Centre

4–5/F, Hong Kong Arts Centre, 2 Harbour Road, Wan Chai; tel: 2824 5330; www.hkac.org.hk; daily 10am–8pm; free; MTR: Wan Chai (exit C), bus: Harbour Road, Fenwick Street; map p.138 A3

The Pao Galleries inside the multi-purpose Hong Kong Arts Centre regularly exhibit works by acclaimed international artists, and are a fine showcase for contemporary art and crafts. The exhibition programme changes frequently and is very mixed, but international and local exhibitions of paintings, photography, crafts and design are staged.

Sam Tung Uk Museum

2 Kwu Uk Lane, Tsuen Wan; tel: 2411 2001; www.heritage museum.gov.hk; Wed–Mon 9am–5pm; free; MTR Tsuen Wan, 5 min walk from exit E; bus: 40;

In striking contrast to the modern high-rise town that now surround it, this Hakka walled village, founded by the Chan clan in 1786 recreates life in the New Territories in the 19th and early 20th centuries.

Restored in the 1980s and declared an historic monument, this gem of a museum displays period Hakka furniture and farming implements. It hosts regular temporary exhibitions on different aspects of the region's folk culture and transformation from farmland to industrial and urban centre.

Sun Yat-sen Museum and Historical Trail

7 Castle Road, Mid-Levels; tel: 2367 6373, http://hk.drsun

yatsen.museum/en/index.php; Mon–Wed and Fri–Sat 10am–6pm, Sun 10am–7pm; entrance charge; MTR: Central, then Mid-Levels Escalator, bus: Caine Road; map p.136 B3

One of Hong Kong's newest museums, dedicated to the life and teachings of Chinese revolutionary Dr Sun Yat-sen. In 1911 Dr Sun, who had studied and worked as a doctor in both Hong Kong and Macau, succeeded in overthrowing the Qing dynasty, and with it some 2,000 years of Chinese autocracy.

Located in the historic Kom Tong Hall, an impressive Edwardian-style residence built for a wealthy local merchant in 1914, the museum's galleries bring the revolutionary activities of the era to life through artefacts, manuscripts, letters, photographs and a well-narrated audio guide, and demonstrate how a tolerant colonial government in Hong Kong indirectly acted as a catalyst for the development of revolutionary activities in China.

The museum is also the starting point for exploring the cluster of sites in Central and Western District that form the **Sun Yat-sen Historical Trail**. These include the shop that was the first

One-Stop Museum Pass

The museum pass, valid for a week (HK$30), allows unlimited admission to seven of Hong Kong's most popular museums: the Hong Kong Museum of Art, the Hong Kong Science Museum, the Hong Kong Space Museum (excluding the Space Theatre), the Hong Kong Museum of History, the Hong Kong Museum of Coastal Defence, the Hong Kong Heritage Museum and the Sun Yat-sen Museum. All seven museums are free on Wednesdays. It is available from participating museums and Hong Kong Tourist Board visitor information centres (see p.38).

meeting place for the 'four desperados' (Sun and his first three co-revolutionaries), and the old site of the College of Medicine for Chinese, where Sun received his medical training in the 1880s.

Pick up a map of the trail at the museum; free guided tours are also available on Saturdays (booking ahead is advisable, through Hong Kong Tourist Board offices or website). They are usually in Cantonese, so check when any are available in English. There is also easy-to-operate audio guide equipment.

University Museum and Art Gallery

University of Hong Kong, 94 Bonham Road, Pok Fu Lam; tel: 2241 5500; www.hku.hk/hku mag; Mon–Sat 9.30am–6pm, Sun 1–6pm; free; bus: 3B, 23, 40, 40M, 103 from Central; map p.136 A3

Easily located by the main entrance of the University of Hong Kong, the highly respected Fung Ping Shan Museum became the University Museum in 1996, with the addition of a new wing. The museum now occupies the whole of the attractive Edwardian Fung Ping Shan building, while the art gallery is in the lower storeys of the TT Tsui Building; a bridge links the two. UMAG's collections have grown to include over 1,000 Chinese antiquities, notably bronzes, ceramics and paintings dating back to the 7th century.

Most prized is the world's largest collection of bronze crosses, produced during the Yuan dynasty by the Nestorians, a Christian sect that arrived in China around AD 600. Also on display are over 300 items of Chinese ceramics and carvings from the world-renowned Tsui collection, lodged in the museum on long-term loan.

Below: Sun Yat-sen Museum.

Music, Dance and Theatre

Be it Chinese or Western, the arts are a significant and growing part of the Hong Kong landscape. Whether your interests run from classical music to pop or contemporary dance, the city offers a wealth of sophisticated performances. Spend a magical evening with the Hong Kong Chinese Orchestra, a night being dazzled by the pyrotechnic shows of global pop superstars or an afternoon at a glitzy Western musical; it is all there for the taking in this East-meets-West artistic hub.

Chinese Arts

Hong Kong Chinese Orchestra

Tel: 3185 1600; www.hkco.org

One of the largest of its kind in the world, the Hong Kong Chinese Orchestra remains Hong Kong's only full-scale professional orchestra dedicated to playing traditional Chinese music. The 85-strong orchestra has performed at many famous venues and festivals around the world, but also appears regularly at the **Hong Kong Cultural Centre** *(see p.74)* and other venues around the Territory. Under the baton of artistic director and principal conductor Yan Huichang, it has taken on the mission of promoting Chinese music worldwide, and its repertoire includes both traditional folk music and contemporary full-scale works, many commissioned for the orchestra. Among its most famous recordings are *The Butterfly Lovers* and *Journey to Lhasa*.

Hong Kong Dance Company

Tel: 3103 1888;
www.hkdance.com

Above: the Hong Kong Dance Company.

A uniquely Hong Kong mixture: the city's special culture and history is a rich artistic source for Hong Kong Dance, whose style vividly coalesces East and West. Committed to maintaining Chinese dance, the company performs both traditional folk dances and dance dramas and entirely original works that freely incorporate Western techniques, and since its foundation in 1981 the HKDC has staged over a hundred productions choreographed by local, mainland and overseas choreographers, to critical acclaim. It adheres to a belief that dance derives from tradition but is not restricted by boundaries; the results are vibrant and spectacular.

Western Dance and Music

BALLET AND CONTEMPORARY DANCE

City Contemporary Dance Company

Tel: 2329 7803;
www.ccdc.com.hk

The flagship of modern dance in Hong Kong, the CCDC is renowned for its distinctive and diverse style of programmes. Founded by choreographer (and still the company's director) Willy Tsao in 1979, it endeavours to rally the best of Chinese talents to create dance in a contemporary Chinese con-

> Check www.discover hongkong.com or the websites of *bc* and *HK* magazines for forthcoming programmes, and www.hk.artsfestival.org for information on the Hong Kong Arts Festival.

Left: Chinese opera still has mass appeal in Hong Kong.

text, and as well as presenting Tsao's own work has nurtured some of the best choreographers in town, including Helen Lai and Mui Cheuk-yin. The company also tours widely, enlightening audiences worldwide with innovative works and reaching around 100,000 people each year.

Hong Kong Ballet
Tel: 2573 7398;
www.hkballet.com
Hong Kong is home to one of the foremost classical ballet companies in Asia. For the past few years the Hong Kong Ballet has served as a cultural ambassador, performing in Europe, North America, Singapore and throughout Greater China. Presenting a broad-based repertoire ranging from classical and neoclassical to contemporary works, and specially-commissioned new works. The company of over 40 dancers – most of whom are from Mainland China – are led by artistic director Madeleine Onne, a former principal ballerina of the Royal Swedish Ballet.

ORCHESTRAL MUSIC
Hong Kong Philharmonic Orchestra
Tel: 2721 2030; www.hkpo.com
Now under artistic director Jaap van Zweden, this acclaimed orchestra is in residence at the **Hong Kong Cultural Centre** (see p.74) from September to July. After enriching Hong Kong's cultural life for over a century the HKPO is one of Asia's leading orchestras, a formidable ensemble of Chinese and international talents. It presents over 150 performances each year, from core symphonic classics to collaboration with Cantopop artists. The orchestra also attracts world-class soloists to perform on the same stage.

Hong Kong Sinfonietta
Tel: 2836 3336;
www.hksinfonietta.org
Hailed as 'one of the world's great small orchestras', the Hong Kong Sinfonietta was founded by music graduates in 1990 with the aim of bringing music closer to the community. Today, under the leadership of music director Yip Wing-sie, the orchestra performs over 70 times a year – mainly at **Hong Kong City Hall** (see p.74) – and is renowned for its impassioned performances, innovative audience development concerts, crossover productions and new commissions. Over the years, the orchestra has collaborated with an illustrious array of international musicians, including Pavarotti and Zukerman, and has been a regular guest at festivals at home and abroad.

Contemporary Music

CANTOPOP
The first generation of Cantonese pop stars – launching

Below: Cantopop stars Orchids Eighteen.

Chinese Opera remains an integral part of Chinese culture and, however alien it may seem at first to most Westerners, it is certainly worth going to see a performance while you are here. In Hong Kong opera performances (Cantonese operas are naturally the most popular) are customary during important festivals on the Chinese calendar. Traditionally, they were put on in temporary bamboo-and-mat theatres in public squares, but they have now moved into Hong Kong's modern venues.

To foreign ears, the high-pitched wails of a Chinese opera, interrupted by deafening gongs and drums, seem bizarre and discordant, but Chinese singers undergo long training to achieve a properly pitched falsetto. Every part of the performance has a special meaning: make-up, movements, props and costume colours identify an actor's age, sex and personality the moment he or she appears on stage.

Most traditional opera performances in Hong Kong form what are known as *sumkung* (eulogy of the gods), as they are performed to celebrate special festivals or the birthdays of different gods. Many are related to Taoism and Buddhism; during the Hungry Ghost Festival, operas are staged intermixed with other ceremonies to expiate the sins of the dead. It is perfectly acceptable for audiences to arrive late, leave early, walk around, chat or even eat during a Chinese opera, which may run from three hours to a whole day. When an actor sings especially well, the audience is expected to respond by shouting out praise and applauding.

Above: extravagant characters from a Chinese opera.

the style quickly dubbed Cantopop – appeared in the mid-1970s. There have been a handful of genuine stars, but the genre is generally dominated by teen idols whose popularity tends to depend more on their looks than their voices.

Foremost in fan-appeal since the early 1990s were the 'Four Heavenly Kings' – Leon Lai, Jackie Cheung, Andy Lau and Aaron Kwok – and pop-rock band Beyond, who broke up in 2005. Female singers are equally ubiquitous, such as Sally Yeh, Kelly Chen, Sammi Cheng and Hong Kong's greatest superstar, Beijing-born 'Heavenly Queen' Faye Wong, who is phenomenally popular across East Asia.

More recent arrivals include Andy Hui, Eason Chan, Yang Mi, MC Jin and Khalil Fong.

Cantopop stars frequently cross over into Hong Kong movies, and have massive followings. Heart-throb singer/actor Leslie Cheung's death in 2003 is still mourned annually – in a suicide jump from the top floor of the Mandarin Oriental hotel – the city was practically paralysed by grief.

A 2008 internet nude-photo scandal revealed more than the industry wanted of a few Cantopop stars, who had previously traded on their 'innocent' image.

JAZZ

The Hong Kong Jazz Association is a non-profit organisation of jazz lovers and professional musicians dedicated to promoting jazz among Chinese communities.

Sadly, a couple of the city's best jazz venues have closed in recent years, but a jazz contingent is included as part of the annual Arts Festival (2012 included Dr John, The Lower 911 and Charlie Haden) and the **Fringe Club** has regular jazz slots.
SEE ALSO NIGHTLIFE, P.79

MUSICALS

Broadway and West End musicals have a big audience in Hong Kong, and touring productions frequently visit the city for runs of a month or so, usually at the **Hong Kong Cultural Centre** or the **Academy for Performing Arts** (see p.74). Major crowd-pullers have included Andrew Lloyd Webber's *The Phantom of the Opera*, *The Sound of Music*, *Saturday Night Fever*, ABBA-based *Mamma Mia!*, *Grease* and *Singin' in the Rain*.

POP AND ROCK

Hong Kong has finally made it onto the international concert circuit. Programming possibilities were long lim-ited by the lack of suitable venues, but the situation has changed since the opening of the **AsiaWorld-Expo Arena** at the end of 2005. This has now hosted Coldplay, Avril Lavigne and Gorillaz, and has been a stop on the world tours of pop diva Lady Gaga. Less stadium-sized acts still tend to play at the Convention Centre or smaller venues in town.

Theatre

Hong Kong Repertory Theatre

Tel: 3105 5930;
www.hkrep.com
Established in 1977, the HKRep is the Territory's leading professional theatre company, with a repertoire covering Chinese and international drama and original local plays. Under its director, US-trained Anthony Chan, the company also pursues an energetic policy of cultural exchanges with mainland China, other Chinese communities and the rest of the world. Produc-tions, presented at the **Hong Kong Cultural Centre** (see p.74) and other venues, are usually in Cantonese or Mandarin, with English sub-titles.

Venues

For the latest programme information visit www.discover hongkong.com, *Where Hong Kong* or *HK* magazines or their websites.

AsiaWorld-Expo Arena
AsiaWorld-Expo, Hong Kong International Airport, Lantau; tel: 3608 8828; www.asiaworld-expo.com; Airport Express from Central
This giant 13,500-seat hall has opened up Hong Kong to a flow of suitably giant-scale pop acts. It is part of the huge AsiaWord-Expo site, right next to the airport.

Fringe Club
2 Lower Albert Road, Central; tel: 2521 7251; www.hkfringe club.com; MTR: Central; map p.137 C2
Housed in what was the 19th century dairy farm's Central ice and cold storage warehouse, the Fringe is

Below: Hong Kong Coliseum.

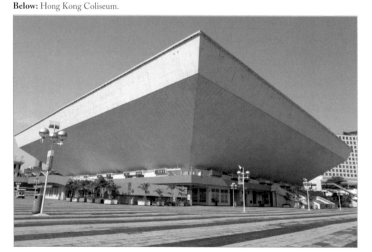

Hong Kong's foremost centre for alternative arts, with a small theatre and studio, galleries and a roof garden-bar that holds around 120 people. The programme is a rich mix, and includes jazz, avant-garde new music and rock.
SEE ALSO NIGHTLIFE, P.79

Hong Kong Academy for Performing Arts
1 Gloucester Road, Wan Chai; tel: 2584 8500; www.hkapa.edu; MTR: Wan Chai (exit C); map p.138 A3
One of the foundation-stones of Hong Kong's cultural effervescence, with courses in every field from TV to Chinese opera, the Academy also contains the Lyric Theatre – used by the Hong Kong repertory and visiting companies – and presents fine concerts by its own students and international musicians.

Hong Kong Arts Centre
2 Harbour Road, Wan Chai; tel: 2582 0200; www.hkac.org.hk; MTR: Wan Chai (exit C); map p.138 A3
As well as containing art galleries and a cinema this multi-purpose venue hosts theatre groups (some in English) and occasional concerts.

Hong Kong City Hall
5 Edinburgh Place, Central; tel: 2921 2840; www.cityhall.gov.hk; MTR: Central; map p.137 D3
City Hall contains a 1,424-seat concert hall and a 463-seat theatre, which hosts Chinese opera and Western music, and many festival and cultural events. There is also an exhibition hall.

Hong Kong Coliseum
9 Cheong Wan Road, Hung Hom,

Right: Hong Kong Arts Centre.

Left: the bustling Hong Kong Arts Centre.

Kowloon; tel: 2355 7234; www.lcsd.gov.hk; bus: 101, 104, 110; map p.135 E3
This inverted-pyramid arena has space for 12,500 people. It is the favourite venue for Cantopop stars, but international acts sometimes make an appearance too.

Hong Kong Convention and Exhibition Centre
1 Expo Road, Wan Chai; tel: 2582 8888; www.hkcec.com; MTR: Wan Chai (exit C); map p.138 A3
AsiaWorld Arena has displaced the Convention Centre from its role as Hong Kong's largest venue, but it still hosts many visiting acts and musicals: David Byrne, Kylie Minogue and Roger Waters have all played here in the past.

Hong Kong Cultural Centre
10 Salisbury Road, Tsim Sha Tsui, Kowloon; tel: 2734 9011; www.hkculturalcentre.gov.hk; MTR: Tsim Sha Tsui; map p.134 B1
Opened in 1989, this giant slab-like structure on the Kowloon waterfront is Hong Kong's premier arts venue, with three fine auditoria and many other facilities. It hosts most performances by the

Above: City Hall hosts many live events.

Urbtix (tel: 2734 9009, www.urbtix.gov.hk) is the official booking service for most events at the major public venues, but a private company, **HK Ticketing** (tel: 3128 8888, www.hkticketing.com), has tickets for several others, including the AsiaWorld-Expo Arena, the Hong Kong Arts Centre and the Fringe Club. Ticket prices vary dramatically: from HK$70 to see an act at the Fringe Club, HK$880 to see Lady Gaga to HK$1,000 to see operatic superstar Renée Fleming perform with the Hong Kong Philharmonic Orchestra. Expect to pay HK$150–250 for a basic seat at a decent performance.

Hong Kong Philharmonic and the Hong Kong Chinese Orchestra and many visiting artists, including musicals. There are also frequent and varied free concerts, especially during the day.

Ko Shan Theatre
77 Ko Shan Road, Hung Hom, Kowloon; tel: 2740 9222; www.lcds.gov.hk; bus: 101, 106, 107, 108, 111
A modern venue popular for Chinese opera, which sometimes hosts pop shows too.

Queen Elizabeth Stadium
18 Oi Kwan Road, Wan Chai; tel: 2591 1346; www.lcsd. gov.hk; bus: 5A, 10; map p.138 C2
An indoor sports hall (hence awful acoustics) that has hosted many gigs by medium-sized international acts. It recently emerged from a major renovation, having reopened in late 2008.

Sha Tin Town Hall
1 Yuen Wo Road, Sha Tin, New Territories; tel: 2694 2509; www.lcsd.gov.hk/stth; KCR: East line to Sha Tin
A product of the Hong Kong

government's plan to decentralise culture in the Territory, this modern multi-space venue hosts a range of traditional Chinese and other performances.

Festivals
Festivals play a big part in Hong Kong's cultural calendar. The **Hong Kong Arts Festival** (tel: 2824 3555; www.hk.artsfestival.org), running through February and

early March, is the main event, which every year features the best Hong Kong and Chinese artists and first-class international performers such as the Moscow Philharmonic, Youssou N'Dour, the Royal Shakespeare Company and Welsh National Opera. Performances are mainly held in City Hall, the Hong Kong Cultural Centre and the Academy for Performing Arts.

Below: Hong Kong Convention and Exhibition Centre.

Nightlife

Big expense accounts, an international status as a trading capital and a large expat community translate into neon-dusted nights of delight in this town of edgy excess. Hong Kong knows how to party well into the early hours every night of the week. So, whether it is international DJs in a monolithic warehouse space, or sweaty moments in a postage-stamp-sized back alley room, there is bound to be something to suit every taste. Just remember, the better you dress, the more you will impress. When it comes to status, the more you work the luxury labels, the more velvet ropes will be brushed aside.

Central and Western: Lan Kwai Fong and SoHo

The younger set mostly heads for the bars and clubs in Lan Kwai Fong while the after-work crowd heads to SoHo (South of Hollywood Road) above Central. The Fong used to be the only real hang-out for Westerners, until the Mid-Levels Escalator opened and breathed new life into what was essentially a quiet local residential neighbourhood. The success of its restaurants, hip boutiques, cafés and bars, creating a whole new shopping, dining and clubbing hub that now spreads along Wyndham Street, Lyndhurst Terrace and

Opening hours and admission charges for nightclubs vary dramatically, and we have only listed information for clubs with a consistent policy. Weeknights are often free, while on weekend nights cover charges are the norm, and special events could make getting in pretty expensive. As far as closing times go, there is little worry in ever getting sent home before dawn.

Above: having a drink in SoHo.

Sheung Wan. SoHo is slightly more chichi and has bags more character. It is easy enough to dip in and out of them both in one evening, and you should certainly try both during your visit.

Wan Chai

Forever associated with *The World of Suzie Wong* tag from the 1960s, Wan Chai has been partying for decades. But if you are prepared to look there are some real finds here. Most notable recently is the new nightlife hub that has mushroomed between Johnston Road and **Star Street**, where a handful of sophisticated bars and restaurants has transformed this once little-known patch of Wan Chai.

Many revellers from Lan Kwai Fong and SoHo cab it to Wan Chai around midnight to finish off the night in more spit-and-sawdust style at venues like **Joe Bananas** *(see p.78)*. While it does have more of a stag or hen night vibe most nights, the number of 'girlie' or 'hostess bars' and other seedier bars in Wan Chai is dwindling. But be on the alert and do not leave your drink unattended.

Kowloon

Although Tsim Sha Tsui does not have the volume of bars that Central does, there is no need for anyone staying on Kowloon to go rushing over to Central for their nightlife fix. Today TST offers far more in the way of choice, not to mention some truly stylish bar-restaurants like **Aqua Spirit** *(see p.95)* – one of the places to be in Hong Kong – and an ever-wider selection along the

Left: Lan Kwai Fong at night.

clubs in town; Friday night is gay night, but the crowd is always pretty mixed.

Devil's Advocate
G/F, 48–50 Lockhart Road, Wan Chai; tel: 2865 7271; www.devils advocate.com.hk; hours vary; MTR: Wan Chai; map p.138 A2
Late-night dancing, big sports screens and a 'sinfully delicious' menu set the scene at this relaxed bar and dance spot, with a slightly cheesy 'devilish' theme.

Dragon-i
UG/F, The Centrium, 60 Wyndham Street, Central; tel: 3110 1222; www.dragon-i.com.hk; daily noon–3pm, 5pm–late; MTR: Central; map p.137 C3
The celebrity haunt of choice is this bar-restaurant-nightclub that has seen everyone from David Beckham to Naomi Campbell grace its hallowed halls. Very expensive, but worth it if you like to party with international jet-setters.

Drop
Basement, On Lok Mansion, 39–43 Hollywood Road, Central; tel: 2543 8856; www.drophk.com;

alfresco Knutsford Terrace. A good selection of bars and pubs can also be found on Ashley Road, or the side streets around Carnarvon Road. Shiny new malls in TST and West Kowloon have added more venues, including new alfresco choices with iconic views, while the restoration of the 19th century Marine Police Headquarters has created some unique venues.

Clubs

Armani/Privé
2/F, 11 Chater Road, Central; tel: 2805 0028; Mon–Sat noon–3pm, 6–11pm, Sun noon–7pm; MTR:

Nightclubs and bars in Hong Kong open and close faster than a tiger out for the kill. What is hot one day could be derserted the next. Stay in the know by checking the listings at **www.hkclubbing.com**. This valuable website posts listings, details on theme nights, reviews and even comments from local residents. Women should especially look out for postings that detail 'Ladies Nights' and other free entry and drink specials.

Central; map p.137 D3
With a name like Armani, you'd expect this bar to be the height of chic – and you'd be right. The place comes into its own after 10pm when the bar vibe turns much more nightclub in style after the international DJs take to the decks. Dazzling outdoor terrace for dinner and drinks.

Beijing Club
2–8 Wellington Place, Central; tel: 2526 8298; www.beijing club.com.hk; Mon–Sat 10.30pm–late; MTR: Central; map p.137 C3
Hong Kong's latest hip addition is this three-storey venue which makes free use of Austrian crystals in its glitzy design. On busy nights members get preferential treatment, so it is best to arrive early if you want to get in.

Club 97
9 Lan Kwai Fong, Central; tel: 2186 1837; www.ninetyseven group.com; Mon–Thur 6pm–2am, Fri 9pm–4am, Sat–Sun 8pm–late; MTR: Central; map p.137 C2
One of the longest-running but still one of the hippest

Right: the city above sleeps while Lan Kwai Fong beats.

Tue–Sun 7pm–late; MTR: Central; map p.136 B3

Low tables, high ceilings, cool sounds and always a queue at the door; Drop also serves the best fresh-fruit martinis in town. A smooth cocktail bar in the early evening, ramping up to a jam-packed party venue at night.

Home Base

LG/F 17–19 Hollywood Road, Central; tel: 2537 1000; Tue–Thur 6pm–6am, Fri–Sat 6pm–9am; MTR: Central; map p.136 C3

The place to go in the early hours of the morning: keep the party going through the night by joining the throngs on the soul-fuelled dance floor, or crash out in the chill-out space, featuring massive leather beds. Open until 9am every weekend.

Joe Bananas

23 Luard Road, Wan Chai; tel: 2529 1811; www.joebananas. com; Mon–Thur noon–4pm, Fri noon–5am, Sat 4pm–5am, Sun 3pm–4am; free; MTR: Wan Chai; map p.138 A2

The 'one and only' Joe Bananas has been around as long as most local partygoers can remember: far from sophisticated, but it sure is fun. Crazy hour prices from opening until 10pm daily. Ladies Night is on Wednesdays, when drinks are free from 10pm–2am.

Kee Club

6/F, 32 Wellington Street, Central; tel: 2810 9000; hours vary; MTR: Central; map p.137 C3

Is that a Picasso I see on the wall before me? Why, yes it is! And that is not the only work of elite art at Hong Kong's most exclusive bar. Dancing does occur – sort of – but most patrons are too busy checking out each other's clothes, wallet and beauty (in that order), and would never risk working up

Hong Kong's members' club scene is burgeoning. There is now a handful of exceptional members' clubs, and not all of them are as off limits to visitors as you may think. The trick is to butter up your highly regarded hotel concierge. Concierges at a clutch of five-star hotels in the city have the connections – and the power – to oil the doors. This is a prime example of the way Hong Kong's village mentality really comes to the fore, and you might as well work it.

a sweat. Go if you can, if only to see how the other half lives just this once. A concierge with connections may be able to get you in.

Mes Amis

83 Lockhart Road, Wan Chai; tel: 2527 6680; Sun–Thur noon–1am, Fri–Sat until 2am; MTR: Wan Chai (exit A1, C), bus: Gloucester and Hennessy roads; map p.138 A2

More of a sports/wine bar than a nightclub, it becomes a true dance spot late in the evening after the wine has been drunk and the rugby and football matches fade from the TVs. Do not expect anything too sleek or chic.

Typhoon

37–39 Lockhart Road, Wan Chai; tel: 2527 2077; daily 4pm–3am; MTR: Wan Chai; map p.138 B3

More pub than club, this typical Wan Chai establishment serves up the usual shooters and happy hour mix to a standard top dance hits soundtrack.

Vertigo

26/F, QRE Plaza, 202 Queen's Road East, Wan Chai; tel: 2575 8980; www.vertigohk.com; Mon–Sat 6pm–3am; MTR: Wan Chai; map p.138 A2

Tournament-quality pool tables, top-quality sound system and sophisticated interiors draw the masses to this 3,000-sq m (32,000-sq ft) venue in the heart of the vibrant and buzzing Wan Chai scene.

Volar

38 D'Aguilar Street, Lan Kwai Fong; tel: 2810 1510; www.volar. com.hk; Mon–Sat 6pm–late; MTR: Central; map p.136 C3

When it opened in 2004, Volar made a huge impression on locals by hiring huge international DJs and spending a fortune on mood-enhancing lighting. You will need to look good to get in, as the velvet ropes are notoriously hard to get behind thanks to some of the city's most picky doormen. Or make a table reservation in advance.

Live Music

All Night Long

9 Knutsford Terrace, Tsim Sha Tsui, Kowloon; tel: 2367 9487; daily 3pm–6am; MTR: Tsim Sha Tsui; map p.135 C2

The bands are mostly Filipino and vary wildly in quality, but you are always guaranteed a good time. And where else can you indulge in your passion for getting down to the best of Wang Chung?

Backstage

1/F, 52–54 Wellington Street, Central; tel: 2167 8985; Mon. 4pm–3am, Tue–Sat noon–1am; MTR: Central; map p.137 C3

Backstage is all about live music. It promotes all genres with one of the most eclectic events calendar of any venue in Hong Kong.

Dusk Till Dawn

76 Jaffe Road, Wan Chai; tel: 2528 4689; Mon–Fri noon–6am, Sat–Sun noon–3am; MTR: Wan Chai; map p.138 A3

Down and dirty live music venue. The bands – playing mostly classic covers – take to the stage around 10pm.

Fringe Club

2 Lower Albert Road, Central; tel: 2521 7251; www.hkfringe. com.hk; Mon–Thur noon– midnight, Fri–Sat noon–2am; MTR: Central; map p.137 C2

The Fringe Club is much more than just a live music venue, this alternative arts space also hosts live performance, art openings, music and more.

Gecko

Ezra Lane, Lower Hollywood Road, Central; tel: 2537 4680; daily 6pm–3am, Fri–Sat until late; MTR: Central; map p.136 C3

Hidden away on an alley off Pottinger Street, this intimate bar with a distinctly Gallic flavour is a haven for art and music lovers. Live jazz acts or DJs somehow squeeze in here most nights.

Grappa's Cellar

Basement Jardine House, 1 Connaught Place, Central; tel: 2521 2582; daily 11am– midnight; www.elgrande.com. hk; MTR: Hong Kong, Central; map p.137 D3

Family-style Italian restaurant also occasionally hosts a truly eclectic range of live music gigs from swing bands and jazz to The Damned and The Wedding Present. Tickets sometimes packaged with drinks or food.

Hard Rock Café

LG/F, LKF Tower, 55 D'Aguilar Street, Lan Kwai Fong, Central; tel: 2111 3777; Sun–Thur 11am–2am, Fri–Sat 11am–4am; MTR Central; map p.137 C3

Packing in a good-natured crowd with its classic mix of American food and live cover bands, Hard Rock Café hits all the right buttons and gets the crowd dancing.

Insomnia

LG/F, 38–44 D'Aguilar Street, Central; tel: 2525 0957; www. lankwaifong.com; daily 9am– 6am; MTR: Central; map p.136 C3

Raucous live music venue that tends to share its acts with All Night Long (see above). Don't expect any-

Above: a fancy-dress partygoer.

Karaoke is extremely popular with locals and should be tried at least once, especially if you are with a group. Private rooms are the way to go, so book ahead and get a room together with your crooning friends. *(See also Bars and Cafés, p.28.)*

thing too ground-breaking except for some of the more original pick-up lines.

Ned Kelly's Last Stand

11A Ashley Road, Tsim Sha Tsui, Kowloon; tel: 2376 0562; daily 11.30am–2am; MTR: Tsim Sha Tsui; map p.134 B1

There is live music nightly (except Sunday) from 9.30pm at this rip-roaring Australian pub. Dixieland sounds are the speciality of this long-standing institution, with hearty, no-frills Aussie food to go with them.

The Wanch

54 Jaffe Road, Wan Chai; tel: 2861 1621; www.thewanch.hk; Mon–Sat 11am–2am, Sun noon–2am; MTR: Wan Chai; map p.138 A3

The Wanch has been the mainstay of Hong Kong's live music scene for over 25 years. It's very tiny though, so is always jam-packed. Live music and jam sessions every night and Sunday afternoons.

Left: live music can be anything from rock cover bands to Cantopop.

79

Pampering

The Chinese are firm believers in the benefits offered by traditional medicine, and both Western and Eastern health treatments abound in Hong Kong. From acupuncture and cupping to t'ai chi and feng shui, Hong Kong has all the traditional Chinese medicine techniques covered. Additionally, the main hotels offer extensive treatments tailored to the tastes (and stresses) of Western business travellers. Whether it is a foot massage in a Chinese-style spa or a full-on splurge at one of the numerous hotel spas, you will certainly not go short of indulgent, invigorating options in this city.

Hotel Spas

Almost all Hong Kong's bigger hotels offer some kind of relaxation and beauty facility, but those listed here are the cream of the crop, and are open to non-residents.

Chuan Spa

Level 41, Langham Hotel, 555 Shanghai Street, Mong Kok, Kowloon; tel: 3552 3510; www.chuanspa.com; daily 8am–10pm; MTR: Mong Kok; map p.132 B3

One of the most impressive and respected luxury spas in Hong Kong, the 41st-floor Chuan Spa has stunning views over Kowloon and offers every conceivable form of holistic pampering. Chuan takes the pillars of traditional Chinese medicine to its heart, and a visit here is a must if Chinese therapies are top of your list. The treatments draw on the five pillars of Chinese medicine – wood, earth, metal, fire and water – and the consultants are trained in Chinese medicine, massage and naturopathy. An opulent range of international treatments is also available.

I-Spa at the Intercontinental Hong Kong

Intercontinental Hong Kong Hotel, 18 Salisbury Road, Tsim Sha Tsui, Kowloon; tel: 2721 1211; www.hongkong-ic.intercontinental.com; daily 8am–10pm; MTR: Tsim Sha Tsui; map p.134 C1

I-Spa was Hong Kong's first *feng shui*-inspired spa, and the pool complex boasts a famous and much-photographed trio of infinity-edge Jacuzzi pools of different temperatures, each one 'bleeding' into the harbour. Half- or full-day programmes are available, as well as a huge choice of Chinese and western treatments. The Jet Lag Relief is a speciality, and you have not lived until Henry 'Magic Toes' (or one of the other expert masseuses) has 'walked' on your back while he hangs from bars on the ceiling. There are dedicated treatments for men, and should you really want to push the boat out, try the Essence of the Orient full-day package. Nearby, the hotel also has an equally lavish fitness suite.

If you start to notice people walking around the streets of Hong Kong with huge yellow bruises up and down their arms and necks, relax: it is likely to be a result of cupping. This ancient form of therapeutic massage involves glass light-bulb-shaped jars being fixed on various points on the body. The ugly residual bruises are a result of the jars being 'pumped' to create a vacuum that is used to draw out impurities. Cupping is quite popular in Hong Kong, and is said to be particularly effective for arthritis sufferers.

OM Spa

3/F Regal Airport Hotel, 9 Cheong Tat Road, Hong Kong International Airport, Lantau; tel: 2286 8888; www.regalhotel.com; daily 10am–11pm; Airport Express from Central

Regal International has spent HK$10 million constructing the sumptuous OM Spa and it offers the prospect of complete recuperation after a long flight. With a Thai-influenced design, it features one of the

Left: an aesthetic retreat.

Roman-style pool is pretty spectacular, and it too offers views across the harbour.

Plateau Spa
Grand Hyatt Hong Kong, 1 Harbour Road, Wan Chai; tel: 2588 1234; www.hong kong.grand.hyatt.com; daily 8am–midnight; MTR: Wan Chai; map p.138 A3
Open to day spa visitors as well as the hotel's guests, this vast 7,500 sq m (90,000 sq ft) spa features 23 treatment rooms, residential Plateau guest rooms, a 50m (165ft) outdoor pool with a poolside grill, a tree-lined courtyard and a gym. It will take you an hour just to absorb the treatment menu. Five-hour relaxation, fitness, aesthetics and culinary programmes are all included.

Day Spas

Charlie's Acupressure & Massage Centre of the Blind
Room 1103, 11/F Chung Sheung Building, 9-10 Queen Victoria Street, Central; tel: 2877 9999; www.acupressuremassage.hk,

city's most extensive massage treatment menus, with more than 30 different options. The spa also contains two Spa Suites, five *cabana*-style treatment rooms, 11 superior treatment rooms and a foot-massage salon. In the Karma residential suite, right beside the main spa, guests can enjoy alfresco massages and use the outdoor whirlpool bath.

Peninsula Spa by ESPA
Peninsula Hotel, Salisbury Road, Tsim Sha Tsui, Kowloon; tel: 2315 3322; http://hongkong. peninsula.com; daily 8am–11pm; MTR: Tsim Sha Tsui; map p.134 C1
The product of collaboration between the august Peninsula Hotel and the world-wide ESPA spa group, this lavish facility is located on the 7th and 9th floors of the hotel. It has its aesthetic roots in classical Chinese design, but heritage aside, everything else about the spa is as cutting edge as is possible. The single and double treatment suites all have en suite showers and other facilities, as well as ESPA's customised foot-ritual seating.

Treatments are a combination of East and West: there is also an Asian Tea Lounge surrounded by a crystal water wall, men's and women's relaxation lounges and male and female thermal suites, each featuring a sauna with hypnotic harbour views. The

Below: Yue Spa *(see p.83).*

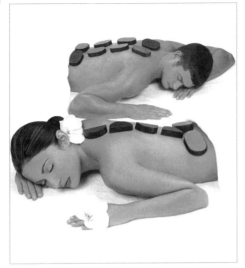

Left: indulge in some traditional Eastern healing.

daily 9.30am–8pm; MTR: Central; map p.136 C3
The Chinese believe that the blind have a heightened sense of touch developed in order to make up for the loss of one of their senses. To help develop a career and generate personal economic independence, many train as massage therapists to take advantage of this belief. You'll find massage parlours with blind masseurs scattered around Hong Kong, but this is one of the better ones. Treatments are no-frills but the quality (and price) is always excellent. Prices start at about HKD$250 an hour.

Iyara Beauty
53 Ship Street, Wan Chai; tel: 2545 8637; www.iyara beauty.com; Mon–Tues, Thur–Fri 2–9pm, Sat–Sun 10am–9pm; MTR: Admiralty Exit F; map p.137 2E/p.138 2A
By appointment only, this day spa is tucked away between Star Street and Queen's Road East. Manipedis are a speciality and Iyara has a good range of massage, body treatments and facials. The two-floor Iyara Beauty is relaxed and informal and welcomes spa-goers with herbal tea by day or wine after 5pm.

ManiPedi
Room 902, Abdoolally House, 20 Stanley Street, Central; tel: 2815 3319; www.manipedi.com.hk; daily 8am–10pm; MTR: Central; map p.136 C3
ManiPedi does what it says – nails, hands and feet – in a contemporary space. If the impeccable service and friendly staff don't have you swooning, the vast choice of nail polishes and leg-reviving massages incorporating flower and plant extracts certainly will. Definitely one for the girls, although there are men's treatments too.

Sense of Touch
G/F, The Ovolo, 2 Arbuthnot Road, Central; tel: 2869 0939; www.senseoftouch.com.hk; Mon–Fri 9.30am–8.30pm, Sat–Sun 10am–10pm; map p.136 C2
Top-class pampering in a professional and relaxed environment and regularly tops the spa awards in Hong Kong. Offering everything from waxing and tanning to facials, mani-pedis and massages,

Spa MTM
Shop A, G/F, 3 Yun Ping Road, Causeway Bay; tel: 2923 7888; www.spamtm.com; Mon–Fri 10.30am–10pm, Sat–Sun 10.30am–8pm; MTR: Causeway Bay; map p.139 D3
MTM is an oasis of calm in the middle of one of Hong Kong's busiest shopping districts. While undergoing a 'skin assessment' and courtesy foot bath you will be asked to select a treatment; try the divine Sakura Revival Therapy. Perfect for wilting shopaholics, the experience begins with a full body mask and a thermal blanket 'wrap' that lets you sweat out your toxins. After cooling down with a cold towel the wrap is washed off in the bath, in preparation for your 90-minute massage.

Sunny Paradise Sauna
341 Lockhart Road, Wan Chai; tel: 2831 0123; daily noon–7am; MTR: Wan Chai; map p.138 B3
Ask any expat-about-town where he or she goes for their sauna, facials or massage and a good number will say Sunny's. This cheap and cheerful option offers no-frills but perfectly good massage services in the heart of Wan Chai: the most popular is the Chinese body massage. The price includes towels, tea and fruit. Separate floors for men and women make this a great budget option for groups of guys or girls who just want to hang out.

Opposite: varnish for colourful fingers and toes.

Tai Pan Reflexology, Beauty and Foot Spa

G/F and Basement, 83 Nathan Road, Tsim Sha Tsui, Kowloon; tel: 2301 1990; daily 8am–1am; MTR: Tsim Sha Tsui; map p.134 C2

After walking down the stairs and across a glass-covered fish pond, you will find a surprisingly large space here, peppered with screens, lanterns and Buddhist paintings, yet somehow the traditional decor is charming and intimate. Ambience aside, the Tai Pan is also reasonably priced: a one-hour session in the massage chair enjoying a foot jet bath followed by reflexology costs around HK$200; a combination head-and-neck massage followed by one-hour foot reflexology is HK$259. Last appointments are around midnight. There is also a branch in Wan Chai, at 441 Lockhart Road.

Victorian Spa

Level 1, Disneyland Hotel, Hong Kong Disneyland Resort, Lantau; tel: 3510 6388; daily 9am–10pm; MTR: Disneyland Resort

Operated by the same people who brought Hong Kong the Paua Spa, this full-service day spa provides an oasis of calm in an otherwise busy resort and amusement park. Inspired by the interiors of the Victorian era, some treatment rooms feature period bathtubs perfect for soaking in.

Yue Spa

3/F, Pearl City Plaza, 22–36 Paterson Street, Causeway Bay; tel: 2576 8369; Mon–Fri noon–9pm, Sat–Sun 10am–7pm; MTR: Causeway Bay; map p.139 D3

The ambience at Yue is relaxingly oriental, with plenty of dark wood, water and Chinese decoration. Organic tea served on arrival, soft music, the calming waft of essential oils and the friendly staff all help set the tone, too. The hefty treatment menu draws on the elements of destiny (nourishment), soil (wraps), metal (circulation), wood (body balance), water (removal of toxins), fire (soothing) and earth. It can be tricky to find, so ask your concierge to write down the full address in Chinese.

Western health treatments abound in Hong Kong, but while here, it is worth trying things the Chinese way. Chinese medicine dates back almost 5,000 years; traditionally, it sees the body as a delicate balance of two opposing forces: *yin* and *yang*. When the balance is upset, it leads to a blockage in the flow of *qi* (pronounced 'chi') or vital energy. Take baby steps and start with a relaxing toe rub: a reflexologist will massage your feet to boost circulation and free the flow of *qi*, and can also provide an all-over diagnosis of your body health. If you enjoy this, another must is an acupuncture session. Acupuncture originated in China almost 2,000 years ago. It works on the principle that there are primary and secondary meridians running through the body, connected by thousands of acupressure points, which can be stimulated by the insertion of fine needles. Acupuncture is one of the most widely used medical procedures in the world, and increasingly accepted in the West, but you will be hard pushed to find such a wide variety of expert acupuncturists as there is in Hong Kong.

Parks and Gardens

Although you will not find parks here on the scale of London's green swathes, or akin to New York's Central Park, Hong Kong has a handful of good, much-appreciated urban parks that are well stocked with facilities including swimming pools and tennis courts. Where you can take five, pause from sightseeing, join the locals in a t'ai chi session or even indulge in a bit of bird-watching. Outside the city there are even more places to spend time with nature, for more on the outdoors, *see Walks and Views, p.126–29.*

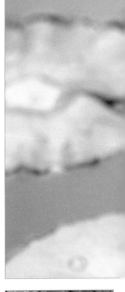

Hong Kong Park

19 Cotton Tree Drive, Central; daily 6am–11pm; free; MTR: Central, bus, tram: Queensway and Hennessy Road; map p.137 D2

Hong Kong Park is an oasis of green amid the surrounding urban landscape. Occupying most of the one-time British Army garrison area known as Victoria Barracks, the park encompasses the **Edward Youde Aviary**, greenhouses, the **Flagstaff House Museum**, the **Hong Kong Visual Arts Centre**, playgrounds, a restaurant and

If you have ever fancied your hand (and feet) at kung fu, head to Kowloon Park on a Sunday afternoon (Sculpture Walk; 2.30–4.30pm), where you will find a variety of traditional kung fu demonstrations taking place, along with performances including ceremonial drumming and lion dances. Onlookers are invited to have a bash, and instructors are happy to guide visitors through the typical movements. It is a great intro duction to Chinese martial arts.

a marriage registry. Amid the vegetation are fine specimens of large trees, which were originally planted by the military. The aviary allows you to walk through a spectacular mix of habitats, with over 150 bird species in a convincing tropical 'rainforest' environment. Twitchers should head to the Conservatory on Wednesdays at 8am for a free two-hour morning birdwatch.
SEE ALSO MUSEUMS AND GALLERIES, P.68

Left: morning exercises at Victoria Park.

Above: Hong Kong Park.

Hong Kong Zoological and Botanical Gardens

Albany Road, Central; tel: 2530 0154, www.lcsd.gov.hk; daily 6am–7pm; free; MTR: Central, bus: 3B, 12, 23, 40; map p.137 C2

Located near the former British governor's residence, these gardens were laid out in 1864 on the northern slope of Victoria Peak. This is a popular spot for morning t'ai chi exercises. The zoo collection occupies a large part of the gardens – particularly on the western side – with about 500 birds, 70 mammals, notably apes, monkeys and lemurs, and 70 reptiles. Many of them are from endangered species, which are being bred successfully in the park.

Left: flora in Hong Kong Park

ing Olympic-sized indoor and outdoor swimming pools children's playgrounds and an open-air Sculpture Garden, Kowloon Park is a tranquil haven at the heart of Tsim Sha Tsui that is especially popular with locals. Others among its many attractions include an aviary and bird lake, where birds range from local sparrows to exotic imported flamingos, wading in landscaped pools, a maze garden, banyan court, and a Chinese garden. Bird watching tour every Friday 7.30–9.30am.

Kadoorie Farm and Botanic Garden

Lam Kam Road, Tai Po, New Territories; tel: 2483 7200; daily 9am–5pm; www.kfbg. org.hk; MTR: Kan Sheung Road or Tai Wo plus bus 64K

Located in the middle of the New Territories at the foot of Tai Mo Shan, KFBG was founded by the Kadoorie brothers in 1951 to provide support for refugees from the Chinese mainland and provide advice on farming techniques. Today it is a centre for conserving plants and indigenous wild animals and con-ducts research into organic farming. Visitors can explore the greenhouses, insect and reptile houses, and follow nature trails along or up the slopes of the farm. The upper peak of the garden is named Kwun Yum Shan (552m/ 1,800ft) and takes about two hours to reach by foot, or hop on the garden's minibus.

Kowloon Park

Kowloon Park Drive, Tsim Sha Tsui, Kowloon; daily 5am–midnight; free; MTR: Tsim Sha Tsui, Jordan; map p.134 B2–3

With a sports complex offer-

Sun Yat-sen Memorial Park

18 Eastern Street North, Sai Ying Pun; daily 24 hours; free; MTR: Sheung Wan; Macau ferry bus terminal; map p.136 A4

Waterfront park with sweeping views of harbour for a break from the city and revive your feet on the pebble trail. Kids can let off steam in a train-themed playground. Indoor swimming pool open year round.

Victoria Park

Between Victoria Park Road and Causeway Road, Causeway Bay; daily 24hrs; free; MTR: Causeway Bay, Tin Hau; map p.139 D/E 3/4

Opened in 1957, Hong Kong's largest park boasts a raft of facilities, including swimming pools, jogging tracks and tennis courts. You can even massage your feet on a special pebble path, and it is naturally another popular early-morning t'ai chi venue. Thousands gather here at festival times, and at weekends the park is full of people exercising, relaxing and simply enjoying the sunshine. Victoria Park also offers the shade of over 5,500 trees.

Below: some use the parks for jogging, others are more sensible.

Restaurants

It has been said that when the Chinese are confronted with something they have never seen before or do not understand, their first impulse is to try eating it. This folk philosophy has helped inspire one of the greatest cuisines the world has known, as well as some of the most bizarre dishes Western visitors have ever seen: from chicken feet to fish eyes, everything is available if you know where to look. It would be a shame not to indulge in the indigenous food on offer, but there are endless restaurants catering for the city's business tourists, putting world cuisine from Thai curries to American burgers on your doorstep.

Central, the Peak and Western

CHINESE

Luk Yu Tea House
24–26 Stanley Street; tel: 2523 5464; daily 7am–10pm; $–$$; MTR: Central; map p.136 C3

This famous and popular teahouse opened in the early 1930s, and is a living piece of Hong Kong history. With its carved wood panelling and doors, ceiling fans, spittoons, marble tabletops, couples booths and stained-glass windows it is also fabulously atmospheric. This is a great place to try the full range of Chinese teas, and is famed for its excellent dim sum (served until 5.30pm).

Lung King Heen
4/F, Four Seasons Hong Kong, 8 Finance Street, Central; tel: 3196 8880; Mon–Sat noon–2.30pm, 6–10.30pm, Sun 11.30am–3pm, 6–10.30pm; $$$$; MTR: Central; map p.137 C4

Spectacular Cantonese food steals the scene from the harbour views this is the first Chinese restaurant in the world to be awarded three Michelin stars. Dim sum and

Above: dim sum made to order.

a swathe of Cantonese delicacies are elevated to a new level with the finest ingredients and elegant presentations. Unlike most Chinese restaurants, Lung King Heen only welcomes children aged over three.

Ning Po Residents Association
4/F, Yip Fung Building, 10 D'Aguilar Street, Lan Kwai Fong; tel: 2523 0648; daily noon–2.30pm, 6–10.30pm; $$; MTR: Central; map p.136 C3

A typical, clattering canteen-style local restaurant hidden inside a commercial building. It is a Hong Kong institution,

and the enormous range of hearty dishes from Shanghai and Ningpo in Eastern China are authentic as is the 80s Chinese décor.

Tim's Kitchen
84–90 Bonham Strand, Sheung Wan; tel: 2543 5919; Mon–Sat noon–3pm, 6.30–10.30pm; $$–$$; map p.136 B4

Excellent Cantonese cuisine with a few fresh twists, Tim's Kitchen has gone from strength to strength winning Chef Lai Yau Tim two Michelin stars. Prices remain reasonable and ambience and dress code is relaxed. Highlights include crab claw with winter melon, pomelo skin with shrimp roe and snake bisque during the winter season. Reservations essential.

Yun Fu
Basement, 43–55 Wyndham Street; tel: 2116 8855;

Prices are for an average three-course meal, with one beer or glass of wine:

$	under HK$150
$$	HK$150–300
$$$	HK$300–500
$$$$	over $500

Left: Chinese restaurant, Central.

Pearl on the Peak
L1, The Peak Tower, 128 Peak Road; tel: 2849 5123; www.the peak.com.hk; Sun–Thur 11.30am–3pm, 6–11.30pm, Fri–Sun 11.30am–3pm, 6pm–12.30am; $$$$; MTR: Central, then Peak Tram
Among the restaurants at the Peak Tower, none is more spectacular than Pearl on the Peak. Inspired by the Melbourne Pearl Restaurant, expect refined Pacific Rim cooking along with sweeping city views through floor-to-ceiling windows. The same 270-degree views can also be enjoyed from a lovely terrace.

Watermark
Star Ferry, Central Ferry Pier 7; tel: 2167 7251; www.cafedeco group.com; Mon–Fri noon–3pm, 6–11pm, Sat–Sun 11.30am–3.30pm, 6–11pm; $$$$; MTR: Hong Kong, Central; Star Ferry
Cuisine is a contemporary continental mix of steaks and seafood, with some remarkable dry-aged steak. Floor to ceiling windows make the most of Watermark's glorious

www.aqua.com.hk; Mon–Fri noon–3pm, 6–11.30pm, Sat–Sun 6–11.30pm; $$$; MTR: Central, then Mid-Levels Escalator; map p.136 C3
Look out for the giant Chinese wooden gate and step into Yun Fu – meaning 'residence on Wyndham Street' – where traditional Chinese wood carvings, buddhas and lanterns guide your way down the scarlet staircase to the basement dining room. Modern interpretations of many dishes from Yunnan, Sichuan, Tibet and Mongolia and China's minorities. An immersive Chinese dining experience, worlds away from the bar scene outside.

FUSION/INTERNATIONAL
Mandarin Grill
Mandarin Oriental Hotel, 5 Connaught Road, Central; tel: 2825 4004; www.mandarin oriental.com; Mon–Fri noon–12.30pm, 6.30–10.30pm, Sat 6.30–11pm, Sun 6.30–9pm; $$$$; MTR: Central; map p.137 D3
One of Hong Kong's best-loved grills, the Mandarin Grill benefited from a Terence

Conran makeover. Although the menu is pricey, the Grill experience is sublime and worth every penny. You might never taste steak this good (fish, pasta and sushi are also on the menu) or be treated to such finely tuned service anywhere in the world. Booking essential.

The Peak Lookout
121 Peak Road, The Peak; tel: 2849 1000; www.peak lookout.com.hk; Mon–Thur 10.30am–11.30pm, Fri 10.30am–1am, Sat 8.30am–1am, Sun 8.30am–11.30pm; $$; MTR: Central, then Peak Tram
The Peak Lookout serves food on a delightful terrace on one of the highest points of the city, alongside the Peak Tower, with, of course, a fabulous view. The menu pleases every imaginable taste with a mix of Chinese, Indian, European and more. It is also great for afternoon tea, or even for a breakfast treat at weekends, after you have worked up an appetite with a Peak stroll.

Right: small local restaurants offer a unique experience.

Vegetarian Options

In Hong Kong you will find restaurants offering cuisines from all over Asia, and the gamut of Western cuisines, not just French or Italian but also Scandinavian, Dutch and Mexican, as well as steakhouses, pizza parlours and kosher food. Vegetarians do not have an easy time here, though. Things are improving, but compared with other Asian countries, such as Thailand and India, there is a noticeable lack of vegetarian choices, and Chinese chefs routinely add chicken or other meat stocks to otherwise 'vegetarian' dishes, to add flavour, so even these may not be what you are looking for. However, there are a handful of restaurants devoted to purely vegetarian cooking. The majority are, naturally, Chinese in their cooking style, often with Buddhist connections, and are thus also frequented by monks. Most of their food should be vegan, and dishes containing eggs are usually labelled on the menu. Indian restaurants are also a good bet, and some hotels also cater for vegetarians, if notified in advance. There are few four-star-and-above chefs in Hong Kong who will not rise to the veggie challenge. For more vegetarian possibilities, in addition to those listed in this chapter, try MSG-free **Kung Tak Lam** in Tsim Sha Tsui, 7/F, 1 Peking Road; tel: 2312 7800, Southern Indian restaurant Branto 1/F 9 Lock Road, TST; tel: 2366 8171; Vegetarian dim-sum restaurant Po Lin Yuen, 69 Jervois Street, tel: 2543 8981. Finally, do not forget the **Po Lin Monastery** on Lantau (*see Temples and Monasteries, p.117*). The **Hong Kong Vegan Society** has a list of vegan-related shops and restaurants at: www.ivu.org/hkvegan.

270-degree vistas, on level P of the Star Ferry pier.

INDIAN

Jashan

1/F, Amber Lodge, 23 Hollywood Road; tel: 3105 5300; www.jashan.com.hk; Mon–Sat noon–3pm, 6–11pm; $–$$; MTR: Central, then Mid-Levels Escalator; map p.136 C3

Modern Jashan offers an extensive menu of Indian cuisine, with dishes from both north and south. A speciality is the exceptional-value lunchtime buffet, and weekend specials but it also offers fine dining in the evening.

Tandoor

Lyndhurst Tower, 1 Lyndhurst Terrace; tel: 2845 2262; daily noon–3pm, 6–10.30pm; $$; MTR: Central, then Mid-Levels Escalator; map p.136 C3

Still one of the most popular curry houses in town, it's especially popular for the lunch buffet. Live Indian music plays every evening to add to the atmosphere.

ITALIAN

208 Duecento Otto

208–214 Hollywood Road, Sheung Wan; tel: 2549 0208 www.208.com.hk; Mon–Sat noon–2.30pm, 6–10.30pm, Sun 10am–4pm, 6–9.30am, $$, bar open until midnight, happy hour 3–6pm

A modern take on rustic Italian at 208. Nibble on thin-crusted pizzas and antipasti, while you sip on a prosecco, select your *secondi* and take in Autoban's outstanding design. Gorgeous Chinese blue and white tiles adorn the walls at this acclaimed open-fronted eatery, credited with shifting the island's dining scene westwards.

Isola Bar and Grill

Levels 3–4, IFC Mall, Finance Street; tel: 2383 8765; www.isolabarandgrill.com; Sun–Thur noon–2.30pm, 6.30–11pm, Fri–Sat noon–2.30pm, 6.30–11.30pm; $$$$; MTR: Hong Kong, Central; map p.137 D4

It is a tough choice: outside on the stunning terrace, or inside in the two-storey, all-white interior. The whiter-than-white and 'understated glam' decor befits the modern Italian menu, thin-crusted pizzas, grills and rustic fare, all of which is served up accompanied by a unique harbour view. The outdoor terrace is one of the best in town, which may well inspire repeat visits. Isobar is open from noon until late so you can linger longer if you like.

Below: rice noodles with vegetables.

Above: savoury samosas, a popular Indian appetiser.

Prices are for an average three-course meal, with one beer or glass of wine:

$	under HK$150
$$	HK$150–300
$$$	HK$300–500
$$$$	over $500

map p.136 C3

Welcome to a Cairo-esque bazaar from the 1930s, with high ceilings, dazzling mirrors, hubble-bubble pipes and even belly dancers. Serving authentic, delicious Egyptian food, Habibi does a great value two-course set lunch. Specialities include *mashwiaat*, Egyptian mixed grill and cold *meze*, all prepared by an Egyptian chef (and all halal). Similar dishes are available deli-style, at the same owners' **Habibi Café**, (112–114 Wellington Street, Central; tel: 2544 3886; map p.136 C3).

Va Bene
17–22 Lan Kwai Fong; tel: 2845 5577; www.vabene ristorante.com; Mon–Sat noon–2.30pm, 6.30–11.30pm, Sun 6.30–11pm; $$$$; MTR: Central; map p.137 C2

The rustically upmarket Va Bene remains one of Hong Kong's most enduringly popular dining spots. It also has about the most genuinely European atmosphere of any Hong Kong restaurant.

JAPANESE
Kiku Japanese Restaurant
Basement, Gloucester Tower, The Landmark, Des Voeux Road East; tel: 2521 3344; daily 11.30am–3pm, 6–10.30pm; $$$$; MTR: Central; map p.137 D2

A properly traditional, pine-panelled restaurant serving *teppanyaki* and sushi delica-cies, *kaiseki*, or *sukiyaki* or *shabu-shabu* set meals. The à la carte menu features Kyoto-style cuisine; grilled cod and eel are especially recommended.

MIDDLE EASTERN
Beirut
27 D'Aguilar Street, Lan Kwai Fong; tel: 2804 6611; daily 11am–2pm, 6pm–late; $$–$$$; MTR: Central; map p.137 C3

Subdued lighting, mosaic mirrors and Lebanese music add to the ambience at Beirut. The restaurant offers an extensive menu of Lebanese specialities, and the homemade hummus is the best in Hong Kong. A fine spot for lunch.

Habibi
1/F Grand Progress Building, 15–16 Lan Kwai Fong; tel: 2544 6198; Mon–Sat 11.30am–11.30pm; $$–$$$; MTR: Central;

SOUTHEAST ASIAN
Good Luck Thai Food
G/F, 13 Wing Wah Lane; tel: 2877 2971; daily 8am–2am; $$$; MTR: Central, then Mid-Levels Escalator; map p.137 C3

Cheap and cheerful dining the way the expats love it: off plastic tables, and in a smelly but very authentic Hong Kong alleyway just off the bar and nightlife hub of Lan Kwai Fong. Famously cheap, and also famous for its *tom yam* soup. Good Luck also owns neighbouring Vietnamese and Malaysian restaurants so grab a seat and take your pick.

Nha Trang
88–90 Wellington Street; tel: 2581 9992; daily 11am–11pm; $$; MTR Central; map p.136 C3

Consistently good Vietnamese fare on a menu that spans the length of the nation, including bun, beef and chicken pho, grilled

89

Classified is benefitting from Hong Kong's new interest in wine and has opened more than half a dozen outlets around town. Charcuterie, artisan cheeses, wines, fine teas, coffees and preserves fill the shelves of this very European-style deli-café, and there are wooden tables surrounded by chalkboards that engender a try-before-you-buy philosophy. Grab a seat, order a cheese platter and pair it with one of a vast selection of quality wines and champagnes. The airy **Press Room** (right) next door (part of the same stable) is a relaxed French brasserie-style restaurant in the one-time print shop of the *South China Morning Post*. Weekend brunch is naturally a strong point. Both are at 108 Hollywood Road, Central; tel: 2525 3444/3454; www.thepressroom.com.hk.

prawn rolls and beef and watercress salad. The flavours zing, the food is fresh and fast, hence queues are an almost permanent feature on the pavement outside.

VEGETARIAN
Life Restaurant & Bar
10 Shelley Street; tel: 2810 9777; www.lifecafe.com.hk; daily 8am–midnight (meals served noon–10.30pm); $$; MTR: Central, then Mid-Levels Escalator; map p.136 C3
A very popular organic vegetarian restaurant where yoga bunnies and gym-toned executives alike munch on freshly made flapjacks and alfalfa, between sips of freshly squeezed passion fruit and carrot juice. Pack a delicious picnic for a day out, by visiting **Life Takeaway Deli** (50C Johnston Road, Wan Chai; tel: 2527 7588).

Wan Chai and Causeway Bay

CHINESE
Che's Cantonese Restaurant
4/F, The Broadway, 54–62 Lockhart Road; tel: 2528 1123, www.jiahongkong.com; Mon–Sat 7–11pm; $–$$; MTR: Wan Chai; map p.138 B3
Look hard for this dim sum specialist where in-the-know locals head when they want to meet friends or close a business deal. Hidden on the fourth floor of an otherwise nondescript office block, Che's transports you into Cantonese heaven through its various dishes that are sure to 'touch your heart'.

Yu Chuan Club
1B, Hundred City Centre, 7-17 Amoy Street; tel: 2838 5233; $$; MTR: Wan Chai; map p.138 A2
A family-run business, this Sichuan 'private dining room' must be booked in advance. Yu Chuan has a well thought-

out menu where diners are charged a fixed price per head for a selection of hot and cold Sichuan dishes.

SOUTHEAST ASIAN
Chili Club
1/F, 88 Lockhart Road; tel: 2527 2872; daily noon–3pm, 6–10.30pm; $–$$; MTR: Wan Chai; map p.138 B3
Mostly Thai in flavouring, the Chili Club actually offers much more than that, dishing up spicy options from across the region. Don't come here for great service as you won't find it. Instead, make a bee-line if hot food at cool prices is your goal.

INDIAN/ITALIAN
Duetto
2/F, Sun Hung Kai Centre, 30 Harbour Road, Wan Chai; tel: 2827 7777; www.chiram.

Opposite: the vegetarians' choice: Life Organic Café.

Right: the atmospheric Hutong *(see p.92).*

com.hk, daily noon–3pm, 6–11pm; $$–$$$; MTR: Wan Chai, Star Ferry; map p.138 B3

Two popular restaurants – one Italian and one Indian – have merged to create this restaurant. Panoramic harbour views and outdoor terrace with good views of the Wan Chai waterfront make this an ideal dining spot. Choose between Italian classics and tandoori, curry and vegetarian specialities, and an all-you-can-eat weekday buffet feast. Monthly comedy club (www.punchlinecomedy.com) with visiting international comedians held here too.

INTERNATIONAL
The Principal

9 Star Street, Wan Chai; tel: 2563 3444; Mon–Sat noon–3pm, 6pm–midnight; $$$; MTR: Admiralty exit via Three Pacific Place link, bus, 1, 5B, 6, 10 to Queen's Road East

A pioneering menu at The Principal takes inspiration from the Canary Islands, so Spanish and African influences abound. Some truly remarkable dishes that let quality ingredients shine amid clever flavour combinations. Spacious and stylish, book ahead for this stellar find.

Dining Room

The Pawn, 62 Johnston Road, Wan Chai; $$$; tel: 2866 3444; MTR: Wan Chai; tram, bus 1, 2, 5B, 10

Modern British cuisine in a restored 19th century pawnshop, Dining Room's menu includes grills, salads and decadent puddings. Hop off the tram and pop in for dinner or a very reasonable set lunch. It's a classy setting for a weekend brunch, or a few bar snacks and cocktails.

KOREAN
Kaya Korean

6/F, 8 Russell Street, Causeway Bay; tel: 2838 9550; daily 11.30am–3pm, 5.30-11.30pm; $–$$; MTR: Causeway Bay; map p.139 C3

Korean restaurants tend to be themey in a bad way. This authentic eatery bucks that trend and serves up the real deal. Don't expect much in terms of ambience. You won't mind when you start eating. The views over Times Square also serve as an inspiring distraction.

Southside

CHINESE
Jumbo Kingdom

Shum Wam Pier Drive, Wong Chuk Hang, Aberdeen; tel: 2553 9111; www.jumbo.com.hk; main restaurant Mon–Sat 11am–11.30pm, Sun 9.30am–11.30pm; $$–$$$; bus: 70, 98 to Aberdeen

These 30-year-old floating restaurants in the middle of Aberdeen harbour are a fun Hong Kong institution: very touristy, but the fantastic over-the-top decor is an attraction in itself. The restaurant offers free sampan rides to the two boats from the Aberdeen quayside, and once on board the food is seafood and other Cantonese favourites:

Prices are for an average three-course meal, with one beer or glass of wine:	
$	under HK$150
$$	HK$150–300
$$$	HK$300–500
$$$$	over $500

signature dishes include Flamed Drunken Shrimp and shark's fin soup with lobster and cognac. The Kingdom also has the more international **Top Deck** space to give it more chic-appeal *(see right)*.

EUROPEAN
Verandah
109 Repulse Bay Road, Repulse Bay; tel: 2292 2821; www.the repulsebay.com; Tue–Sat noon–2.30pm, 6.30–10.30pm, Sun 11.30am–2.30pm, 3.30–5pm, 6.30–10.30pm; $$$; bus: Repulse Bay from Central bus station

With its whirring ceiling fans, metres of wood and rarified atmosphere, this is an atmospheric survivor from the colonial era, with a stunning sea view. It is also one of Hong Kong's best and most popular weekend brunch venues, although lunch, afternoon tea and dinner are just as enjoyable. It makes a good stop-off en route to Stanley, but book as far ahead as possible for weekends.

Saigon at Stanley
Shop 101, 1/F Murray House; tel: 2899 0999; daily noon–11pm; $$$; bus to Stanley

Situated in historic 19th-century Murray House this restaurant captures well an air of a bygone era in Saigon in its decor, while offering contemporary Vietnamese cuisine.

FUSION
Top Deck
Shum Wam Pier Drive, Wong Chuk Hang, Aberdeen; tel: 2552 3331; www.cafedecogroup.com; Tue–Thur 6–11.30pm, Fri 6pm–12.30am, Sat 11.30am–12.30am, Sun 11.30am–11.30pm; $$–$$$; bus: 70, 98 to Aberdeen

Top Deck bills itself as Hong Kong's first 'lifestyle' restaurant, and is an alfresco alternative to the boisterous **Jumbo Kingdom** on the lower decks *(see p.91)*. A bar and lounge is housed under a dramatic three-storey Chinese pagoda roof, and this opens onto the main dining area, and a broad outdoor sun deck. Soak up the Southside views and atmosphere while relaxing in a couch or deck-chair. The menu is an eclectic Chinese, European and pan-Asian mix: Sunday brunch is a speciality, and comes with unlimited bubbles for adults.

Kowloon

AMERICAN
Ruth's Chris Steakhouse
Empire Centre, 68 Mody Road, Tsim Sha Tsui East; tel: 2366 6000; www.ruthschris.com; daily noon–3pm, 6.30–11pm; $$$; MTR: East TST, Hung Hom, bus: Salisbury Road; map p.135 D2

If you are a carnivore craving a juicy steak, this American chain, serving cuts of fillet, strip, rib-eye, porterhouse and T-bone, should hit the spot. Other mains include tuna, chicken, lamb chops and lobster, and salads and sandwiches are also available. Another branch is in the Lippo Centre, 89 Queensway, Central; tel: 2522 9090.

CHINESE
Hutong
28/F, One Peking, 1 Peking Road, Tsim Sha Tsui; tel: 3428 8342; www.aqua.com.hk; daily noon–3pm, 6pm–late; $$$$; MTR: Tsim Sha Tsui; map p.134 B1

Below: stir-fry with beef and vegetables.

Above: Jumbo Kingdom.

One floor down from the same owners' sleekly international **Aqua** *(see opposite)*, Hutong is just as exquisitely designed, but this time reminiscent of an ancient family courtyard in one of Beijing's fast-disappearing *hutongs* (courtyard houses). The restaurant has atmosphere in spades, as well as fabulous views. The food – refined modern variations on North Chinese cuisine – is superb; dishes include crispy boned lamb ribs Hutong-style, bamboo clams steeped in Chinese rose wine and chilli *padi*, crispy soft shell crab with Sichuan red pepper and scallops with fresh pomelo.

Jade Garden
4/F, Star House, 3 Salisbury Road, Tsim Sha Tsui; tel: 2730 6888; Mon–Sat 11am–4pm, 6–11pm, Sun 10am–4pm, 6–11pm; $–$$; MTR: Tsim Sha Tsui; map p.134 B1

Jade Garden offers excellent dim sum until 5pm – order from the English menu, rather than deal with the trolley staff – and beautiful harbour views.

Peking Garden
3 Salisbury Road; tel: 2845 8452; Mon–Sat 11.30am–3pm, 5.30–11.30pm, Sun 11am–3pm, 5.30–11.30pm; $$; MTR: Tsim Sha Tsui; map p.134 B1
This lively restaurant specialises in northern Chinese dishes. Watch fresh noodles being made each evening, and enjoy the Peking Duck-carving exhibitions and Beggar's Chicken clay-breaking ceremonies. There are several other branches, among them those at the **Alexandra House**, 6 Ice House Street, Central; tel: 2526 6456, and at 500 Hennessy Road, Causeway Bay; tel: 2577 7231.

Spring Deer
42 Mody Road, Tsim Sha Tsui East; tel: 2366 4012; daily noon–3pm, 6–11pm; $$$; MTR: Tsim Sha Tsui, bus: Salisbury Road; map p.135 C2
There is nothing fancy about Spring Deer, but this Beijing-style restaurant and its team of senior waiters is a local institution for Peking Duck and other northern specialities, and a favourite among those in-the-know. It is handily located too, around the corner from Nathan Road. Book ahead because it is always packed.

EUROPEAN
Finds
1/F The Luxe Manor, 39 Kimberley Road, TST; tel: 2522 9318; www.finds.com.hk; Mon–Thur 11pm; $$$; MTR: TST, Joradan, bus to Nathan Road; map p.134 C2
An acronym of Finland, Iceland, Norway, Denmark and Sweden, the Finds menu offers a mélange of specialities from the Nordic region. It is also a very cool place to dine, with a fabulous wooden

93

You are spoilt for choice when it comes to dining with a view in Hong Kong. On the south side of Hong Kong Island, try the **Verandah** at Repulse Bay *(see p.92)* for a spectacular harbour view, or the eateries along Stanley Main Street. Alternatively, take a ferry to Lamma or Cheung Chau for their harbour-side seafood restaurants. On clear nights, **The Peak Lookout** *(see p.87)* and other restaurants on Victoria Peak offer breath-taking views. **Felix** at the Peninsula *(see opposite)* and **Aqua** at One Peking Road *(see below)* and the Ritz-Carlton Hong Kong are the big hitters in Kowloon. Book in advance.

deck for pre-dinner cocktails and a great location near Knutsford Terrace. Service is attentive, and the quality high.

Bistro on the Mile

Holiday Inn Golden Mile, 50 Nathan Road, Tsim Sha Tsui; tel: 2315 1118; www.golden-mile.com; daily 8am–11pm; $–$$; MTR: Tsim Sha Tsui; map p.134 C1

Good-value international fare both buffet-style and à la carte. A good place to go if you want to get away from the bustle of Nathan Road but still want to soak in the view of the street below.

Jimmy's Kitchen

G/F Kowloon Centre, 29 Ashley Road, Tsim Sha Tsui; tel: 2376 0327; www.jimmys.com; daily noon–2.30pm, 6–11pm; $$; MTR: Tsim Sha Tsui; map p.134 B2

One of Hong Kong's oldest restaurants, open since the 1930s, wood-panelled Jimmy's specialises in British and European food, but also has curries and a variety of other Asian dishes. There is also a Jimmy's in the South China Building, 1–3 Wyndham Street in Central; tel: 2526 5293.

FRENCH

SPOON by Alain Ducasse

Intercontinental Hong Kong, 18 Salisbury Road, Tsim Sha Tsui; tel: 2313 2323; www.hongkong-ic.intercontinental.com; Tue–Sun 6–11pm, Sun noon–2.30pm; $$$$; MTR: Tsim Sha Tsui; map p.134 C1

Floor-to-ceiling windows and spectacular views are the icing on multi-Michelin-starred Ducasse's cake in this restaurant, his first Asian venture. A ceiling installation of hand-blown Venetian glass spoons barely detracts from the pick 'n' mix menu, based on the idea that diners can combine different culinary traditions and flavours: the perfect choice for those who like to graze.

FUSION

Aqua

29–30/F, One Peking, 1 Peking Road, Tsim Sha Tsui; tel: 3427 2288; www.aqua.com.hk; Mon–Sat noon–2.30pm, 6–11pm, Sun noon–3.30pm, 6–11pm, bar Thur–Sun 5pm–1 or 2am; $$$$; MTR: Tsim Sha Tsui; map p.134 B1

A jaw-dropping must-see, Aqua is, quite simply, where Hong Kong is at. It is made up of **Aqua Roma** (Italian) and **Aqua Tokyo** (Japanese)

Prices are for an average three-course meal, with one beer or glass of wine:
$ under HK$150
$$ HK$150–300
$$$ HK$300–500
$$$$ over $500

R

94

Left: the view from Peak-top restaurants.

INDIAN

Gaylord

1/F, Ashley Centre, 23–25 Ashley Road, Tsim Sha Tsui; tel: 2376 1001; www.chiram.com.hk; daily noon–2.30pm, 6.30–11pm; $$$; MTR: Tsim Sha Tsui; map p.134 B1

This Kowloon Indian has been around since 1972 and serves North and South Indian cuisine, with plenty of seafood and vegetarian dishes. The decor is bland, but live music is a nightly feature and the lunch and dinner buffet menus are good value.

AUSTRALIAN

Black Stump Australian Grill & Bar

1 Knutsford Terrace, Tsim Sha Tsui; tel: 2721 0202; Mon–Fri noon–3pm, 5pm–1.30am, Sat 5pm–3am, Sun 5pm–12.30am; $$; MTR: TST; map p.134 C3

Casual outdoor dining in a modern Australian-style bar, with premium seafood and grilled Aussie specialties – from kangaroo to wagyu steaks. Top place to take in the Knutsford Terrace scene.

ITALIAN

Angelini

Mezzanine Level, Kowloon Shangri-La Hotel, 64 Mody Road, Tsim Sha Tsui; tel: 2733 8750; www.shangri-la.com; daily noon–2.30pm, 6–11pm; $$$$; MTR: Tsim Sha Tsui; map p.135 D2

Ask any local where the best Italian restaurant is in Hong Kong and chances are they will point you here. Less flashy than other establishments in the city, it places its focus on the freshness of its ingredients and the very refined levels of its service.

Fat Angelo's

Shop B, Basement, The Pinnacle,

on the 29th floor and the mezzanine **Aqua Spirit** bar on the 30th, accessed by a sultry mirrored catwalk; whichever you come for, Aqua is all about high chic, glamorous decor and staggering views through double-storey windows.

Felix

28/F, Peninsula Hotel, Salisbury Road, Tsim Sha Tsui; tel: 2315 3188, http://hongkong. peninsula.com; restaurant daily 6–11pm, bar 5.30pm–1.30am; $$$$; MTR: Tsim Sha Tsui; map p.134 C1

This restaurant-cocktail bar is not to be missed: the marvellous view and the striking Philippe Starck design are as memorable as the delectable Pacific Rim fusion cuisine. Visit for a cocktail at

the bar if nothing else, but dress up.

MOS Burger

Shop 1, L4A Langham Place, 8 Argyle Street, Mong Kok; tel: 3514 4301; daily noon–midnight; $; MTR: Mong Kok; map p.132 B3

The second branch of the trendy Japanese burger chain – sticky organic rice replaces the bread bun for some burgers. MOS feels like a healthier alternative for fast food especially if you opt for their seafood rice burger 'cake' of scallops, veg and prawns. The plain old beef version and tasty *tepanyayki* burgers are also available. If the queues are too much, Langham Place has lots of great little food outlets to discover on its maze of levels.

95

With both the Chinese and their British colonisers batty about tea, it is hardly surprising that afternoon tea is a much-loved tradition shared by locals, expats and tourists alike. When in Hong Kong, you should experience high tea at least once in your stay. Popular hotel venues include the **Peninsula**, **Mandarin Oriental**, **InterContinental**, **The Langham** and **Grand Hyatt**. Be sure to push the boat out, since you will only be saving a small amount to downgrade, and some things really are worth doing properly. Britannia may no longer rule the roost, but you could be forgiven for thinking otherwise when you step into the venerable Peninsula hotel (see p.60). The classical grandeur of the lobby and the string quartet set the scene, while the generously laden cake stand and coffees and loose-leaf teas, served in bone china crockery, put many of Britain's own set afternoon teas to shame. You will also pay about half the price London's top hotels charge for the privilege. Afternoon tea at 'The Pen' is an Asian institution, and well worth crossing the harbour for (served daily, 2–7pm). Dress respectfully for tea at the grande dame of HK hotels.

8 Minden Avenue, Tsim Sha Tsui; tel: 2730 4788; www.fatangelos.com; daily noon–midnight; $$; MTR: Tsim Sha Tsui; map p.134 C1
Friendly, uncomplicated, American-style Italian restaurant, dishing up huge portions of pasta favourites that feed up to eight people. Family-style dining, with a children's activity menu. It can also be a romantic setting, with its checked tablecloths and wine served in tumblers. Second branch in the **Panda Hotel**, Tsuen Wan; tel: 2409 8448.

JAPANESE
Nobu
Intercontinental Hong Kong, 18 Salisbury Road, Tsim Sha Tsui; tel: 2313 2323; www.hongkong-ic.intercontinental.com; daily noon–2.30pm, 6–11pm; $$$$; MTR: Tsim Sha Tsui; map p.135 C1
Yawning views of the harbour and city skyline are on a par with legendary miso-flavoured cod and Nobu's new-style sashimi. The waiting list is long, but if you fail to bag a table try the small sushi bar with its nine non-bookable stools, or retreat with sake martinis to the sexy lounge bar clad in 7,700 river rocks, which shares the same vistas.

SOUTHEAST ASIAN
Lee Kam Kee Vietnamese Restaurant
498–500 Nathan Road, Yau Ma Tei; tel: 2781 2028; daily 11.30am–11pm; $–$$; MTR Yau Ma Tei
A fresh clean diner opposite MTR exit C. Lee Kam Kee was one of Hong Kong's first Vietnamese restaurants in the 90s. It offers a spread of dishes such as claypot curry chicken with French bread, a variety of fresh rice paper rolls, *cha lua* (sausage), shrimps and green papaya salad and 19 types of *pho* with rice noodles.

VEGETARIAN
Light Vegetarian Restaurant
G/F, New Lucky House, 13 Jordan Road, Yau Ma Tei; tel: 2384 2833; daily 11am–11pm; $; MTR: Jordan; map p.134 C4
The menu here offers lots of dishes based on Cantonese favourites, but in vegetarian form: rice noodles, *ho–fun*, *udon*, noodles in soup, Chinese congee and imitation meat dishes. Vegetarian dim sum is available to eat in or take away.

New Territories and Outer Islands
CANTONESE
Genuine Lamma Hilton Restaurant
Lot 584, G/F, Sok Kwu Wan, Lamma Island; tel: 2982 8220; daily 11.45am–9pm; $$; Central Pier 4 Sok Kwu Wan
There are two Hiltons in Sok Kwu Wan, and neither is genuine. Food is authentic Cantonese though, with the emphasis on seafood and this family-run restaurant has one of the most pleasant open locations away from the main drag as you walk south. Look for the jetty for the Fishing Fisherfolk museum.
Sampan Seafood Restaurant
16 Main Street, Yung Shue Wan; Lamma; tel: 2982 2388; Ferry; $–$$

Prices are for an average three-course meal, with one beer or glass of wine:	
$	under HK$150
$$	HK$150–300
$$$	HK$300–500
$$$$	over $500

Right: tradition meets modern.

One of half a dozen good alfresco seafood restaurants in Yung Shue Wan, the Sampan also serves dim sum until 11am. Simply go up to the counter, peek in the baskets and order what takes your fancy. For lunch and dinner, there's a full Cantonese menu. Enjoy harbour views and take in village life while feasting. Huge tanks of live fish and crustaceans both entertain and sustain diners.

FRENCH/INTERNATIONAL
One-thirtyone
131 Tseng Tau Village, Sai Kung; tel: 2791 2684; www.one-thirty-one.com; Tue–Sun 7–11pm, Sat–Sun noon–3pm; reservation only; $$; MTR: University, then taxi
If you have a special occasion to celebrate while in Hong Kong, and the weather is looking fine One-thirtyone is perfect. Food is as superb as the setting – European-inspired 'country fine-dining' in a remote cove surrounded by majestic mountains. Fixed price menu for dinner or lunch at weekends.

TURKISH
Bahce Turkish Restaurant
Unit 19, Mui Wo Centre, Mui Wo, Lantau; tel: 2984 0221; daily 12pm-11pm; $$; Ferry
Authentic Turkish cuisine in an unassuming little restaurant, close to Mui Wo's ferry terminal. Order a generous mezze platter and peruse the menu for Turkish-style kebabs.

FUSION
The Stoep
32 Cheung Sha Lower Village, Lantau Island; tel: 2980 2699; www.thestoep.com; Tues-Sun 10am-11pm; $$$; Bus 1, 2, or 4 from Mui Wo Ferry Terminal;
Laid-back alfresco restaurant on the beach, serving a mix of Mediterranean and South African specialities. Always plenty of meat sizzling on the *braai* (grill), to keep the carnivores happy, with cold beers, wine and sangria by the jug.

SRI LANKAN
AJ's Sri Lankan Cuisine
14 Sai Kung Hoi Pong Street, Sai Kung; tel: 2792 2555; Mon 5.30–11pm, Tue–Fri 11am–3pm, 5.30pm–11pm, Sat–Sun 11am–11pm; $$
A rare opportunity to savour the subtle flavours of Sri Lanka, AJ's has an extensive menu of Sri Lankan dishes including hoppers, curries, a host of vegetarian and non-vegetarian fare and devilled dishes.

Below: a huge variety of food is available.

97

Shopping

Shopping in Hong Kong is a rich, varied, seven-days-a-week pursuit. Atmospheric street markets contrast with flagship designer stores, local 'lanes' and cheap-and-cheerful factory outlets selling everything from cut-price trainers to affordable chinoiserie. There are great sales with big discounts, and the summer sales offer visitors fantastic deals on designer fashion labels. Whether it is international styles, home-grown design, Chinese antiques or high-tech electronics, there is something here to satisfy every whim. The sheer variety of products makes Hong Kong a unique shopping experience.

Shopping in Hong Kong

Hong Kong Chinese love to shop. Their appetite for designer fashion labels, gadgets and the latest… well, anything, is insatiable. There is more acreage of glittering multi-levelled malls than you can visit in a month. The shopping experience is not restricted to malls, however. There are street markets to discover, jostling 'lanes' to explore and characterful antiques shops and boutiques.

Although not quite the bargain haven it once was, Hong Kong offers much in the way of variety and keen pricing and lots of local colour.

Shopping Areas

CENTRAL AND THE PEAK
Central and neighbouring Admiralty are known for big department stores, brand-name luxury goods, designer labels, malls (including **Pacific Place** and **IFC Mall**) and smaller but still glittering shopping centres, such as **Chater House**, **Prince's Building**. Numerous boutiques compete with each other along Stanley and Wellington streets and Lyndhurst Terrace.

But there is plenty in the way of character shopping here too. Head for **The Lanes** (officially **Li Yuen** streets, **East** and **West**), two parallel streets between Queen's Road Central and Des Voeux Road Central that are lined with stalls and shops selling and repairing watches, luggage, clothes and costume jewellery.

Further up the steep slopes inland (easily reached via the Central-Mid-Levels Escalator), is the starting point of Hong Kong's **SoHo** (South of Hollywood Road), the most interesting shopping zone in town. Alongside trendy bars and restaurants in this eclectic neighbourhood are local fashion designers, independent jewellers, quirky homeware stores and vintage boutiques, particularly along, **Staunton**, **Elgin** and **Gough** streets.

SHEUNG WAN
Sheung Wan, west of Aberdeen Street, is one of the most atmospheric parts

Below: colourful buys on The Lanes.

Left: Stanley Market antiques.

into locals' daily shopping. At the other end of the continuum, up-and-coming **Star Street** houses lifestyle boutiques, home-ware shops, galleries and cafés.

Causeway Bay is far more hectic. Try to stand still outside **Sogo** on Hennessy Road on a Saturday afternoon and you may well be carried along by a sea of shoppers riding on a gargantuan wave of designer shopping bags; the 'Sogo junction' around Causeway Bay MTR station is home to some of the world's most expensive retail space. As well as glitzy multistorey malls (**Times Square**, **Island Beverley**, **Lee Gardens**), Causeway Bay also has open-air markets selling clothes and costume jewellery, an abundance of cosmetics outlets and shops specialising in shoes, computer equipment and cutting-edge young fashion (especially **Fashion Walk** and Island Beverly malls). This really is 'shopping central' in every sense of the word.

KOWLOON

Kowloon's major artery, **Nathan Road**, ambitiously dubbed the **Golden Mile**, is

Below: hand-carved *chops*.

Opening Hours

Shopping hours vary, but in the main mall shopping starts at around 10am–11am and goes on to 9pm. Shops in the major shopping districts of Causeway Bay and Tsim Sha Tsui stay open later, until 9.30/10pm, and the major markets keep going until at least 10pm, often later. As a rule of thumb, shops in Central and Western open 10am–6.30pm; Causeway Bay and Wan Chai 10am–9.30pm (or later); Tsim Sha Tsui, Yau Ma Tei and Mong Kok 10am–10pm and Tsim Sha Tsui East 10am–7.30pm. Avoid weekday lunchtimes and weekends if you do not like crowds, and do not expect Sunday to offer any respite from credit card temptation. Shopping in Hong Kong is every bit a seven-days-a-week affair.

of Hong Kong and still a centre of traditional Chinese street life. **Western Market** (see p.103) is one of its most accessible hubs. Head south and west of here, across streets like **Jervois** and **Wing Lok Street**, packed with

scores of shops selling bizarre traditional medicines and unrecognisable dried seafood. You will come to **Hollywood Road** and its web of side streets stuffed with antiques, carpet and furniture shops, including **Cat Street Bazaar**, the popular name for **Upper Lascar Row**, a great spot for local ambience with a string of shops and stalls selling antique watches, coins and stone carvings.

Man Wa Lane, east of the MTR station between Queen's Road and Des Voeux Road, is the place to find a Chinese *chop* – a traditional hand-carved personal seal.

WAN CHAI AND CAUSEWAY BAY

Although not a major shopping district, **Wan Chai** is home to trendy furniture stores and a few traditional rattan and Chinese furniture stores along Queen's Road East. **Spring Garden Lane Market** (see p.102) has some cheap and cheerful clothes and toys, but best of all it also connects to the area's fascinating wet and dry markets, for insight starting to live up to its name as gold and jewellery stores targeting mainland tourists thrive, and glittering new malls spring up. Kowloon is also home to the 500-shop **Harbour City**, Hong Kong's largest mall, **The One**, **iSquare**, 'art mall' **K-11** and **One Peking Road** are all packed with fashion stores, luxury brands and chic restaurants. Further north in **Mong Kok**, the glass-and-metal **Langham Place** rises from a warren of backstreets like a vision of the future, with 300 shops spread over 15 floors.

There are plenty of bargains to be had in the grid of side streets that fan out to the east of Nathan Road. Explore the world of washable silk along **Mody Road**, or head to **Granville Road** for outlets loaded with export overruns and bargain fashion. Kowloon is also famous for its specialist street markets, selling everything from clothes and flowers to goldfish and jade.

Malls

Hong Kong has some of the largest, most all-out dazzling retail temples on the planet. The giant mega-malls are natural attention grabbers, but hip, more individual and often quirky fashions and a

less predictable experience can often be found in tiny shops in the many smaller malls around town.

Fashion Walk
Kingston and Cleveland streets, Causeway Bay; MTR: Causeway Bay; map p.139 D3
Pedestrianised streets rather than a true mall, but lined by restaurants and stylish small boutiques.

Harbour City
5 Canton Road, Tsim Sha Tsui, Kowloon; MTR: Tsim Sha Tsui; map p.134 B2
The biggest of all Hong Kong's malls: actually five interconnecting malls, including the Ocean Centre and Ocean Terminal, with just about every brand and store represented.

IFC Mall
8 Finance Street, Central; www.ifc.com.hk; MTR: Central, Hong Kong Airport Express; map p.137 D4
The gleaming mall at the heart of Hong Kong's showpiece IFC development has drawn towards it all the big fashion names, a Lane Crawford department store and a giant Apple store.

Island Beverley
1 Great George Street, Causeway Bay; MTR: Causeway Bay; map p.139 D3
The favourite mini-mall of

Should you encounter problems while shopping in Hong Kong, register a complaint with the **Hong Kong Tourism Board's hotline** (tel: 2508 1234) or the **Consumer Council** (tel: 2929 2222; www.consumer.org.hk). When buying electrical goods, try to obtain an international guarantee, not just a local one.

Hong Kong's young and hip, packed with 70 micro-outlets for local, Japanese or European fashion. Many shops only open after midday.

The Landmark
16 Des Voeux Road, Central; MTR: Central; map p.137 D3
Vast mall in the heart of Central, packed with grand luxury brand names.

Lee Gardens
33 Hysan Avenue, Causeway Bay; MTR: Causeway Bay; map p.139 D2
Relatively low-key mall that nevertheless hosts Chanel, Dior and other upmarket labels. The recently opened Lee Gardens 2 has several good shops for children.

One Peking Road
1 Peking Road, Tsim Sha Tsui; MTR: Tsim Sha Tsui; map p.134 B1
The spectacular One Peking Road skyscraper, home of restaurants like **Aqua**, has a luxury fashion mall at its foot.
SEE ALSO RESTAURANTS, P.94

Pacific Place
88 Queensway, Admiralty; www.pacificplace.com.hk; MTR: Admiralty; map p.137 E2
Huge, four-level mall, with branches of many major stores.

Prince's Building
Chater Road, Central; MTR: Central; map p.137 D3
Medium-sized mall, known for top-range fashion and jewellery labels plus interesting boutiques selling art, antiques and gifts.

Below: The Landmark.

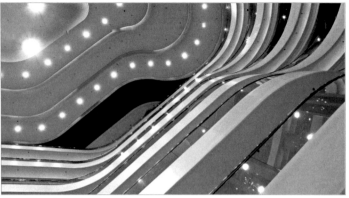

Above: Times Square shopping mall.

Times Square

Russell Street, Causeway Bay; www.timessquare.com.hk; MTR: Causeway Bay; map p.139 C3
Another blockbuster-size mall, with plenty of fashion names, but also a big food court and electronics stores.

Department Stores

Western-style and Japanese department stores – often installed in the main malls – are big hitters in Hong Kong's retail game. Chic and sleek **Lane Crawford** is Hong Kong's equivalent to Bloomingdale's or Harrods, ie classy and expensive. **Harvey Nichols** is a big hit in Hong Kong with stores in The Landmark and Pacific Place.

The Japanese stores **Seibu** in Mongkok and **Sogo** in Causeway Bay have a loyal following.

Lane Crawford

Pacific Place, 88 Queensway, Admiralty; tel: 2118 3668; www.lanecrawford.com; daily 10am–9pm; MTR: Admiralty; map p.137 E2
Founded in 1850, this colonial-era store has adapted very well to modern times. Other large branches are at the IFC mall, Times Square and Harbour City.

Marks & Spencer

Times Square, 1 Matheson Street, Causeway Bay; tel: 2923 7970; www.marksandspencer.com; Mon–Fri 10.30am–8.30pm, Sat–Sun 10.30am–8pm; MTR: Causeway Bay; map p.139 C23
Other M&S branches are at Central Tower, Queen's Road, Central, and at Harbour City.

Sincere

173 Des Voeux Road Central, Sheung Wan, Western; tel: 2544 2688; www.sincere.com.hk; daily 10am–7.30pm; MTR: Sheung Wan; map p.136 C4
Long-established store with international fashion and other products and Chinese specialities, at down-to-earth prices. Also branches in Kowloon.

Sogo

555 Hennessy Road, Causeway Bay; tel: 2833 8338; www.sogo.com.hk; daily 10am–10pm; MTR: Causeway Bay; map p.139 D3
Japanese-style department store that seems to sell everything, with a choice of cute cafés in the basement. Also at 12 Salisbury Road, Tsim Sha Tsui.

Wing On

211 Des Voeux Road Central, Sheung Wan, Western; tel: 2852 1888; www.wingonet.com; daily 10am–7.30pm; MTR: Sheung Wan; map p.136 C4
Another long-running, great-value Hong Kong store, with a huge range of stock, from electronics to traditional *cheongsam* dresses. There are four more Wing On stores around Hong Kong.

Markets

Flower Market

Fa Yuen Street, Mong Kok, Kowloon; daily 7am–7.30pm; MTR: Prince Edward (exit B1); map p.132 B4
Exquisitely colourful, Kowloon's flower market sells everything from Dutch tulips to exotic orchids. As usual, fortune plays a part: particular blooms and plants are associated with different festivals, especially Chinese New Year.

Goldfish Market

Tung Choi Street, Mong Kok, Kowloon; daily 9am–11pm; MTR: Prince Edward (exit B1); map p.132 B4
Aquariums are popular in Hong Kong because of their perceived luck-bringing qualities, so long as they are properly positioned in the home. Mong Kok's Goldfish Market stocks fish, corals, exotic amphibians and tanks.

Jade Market

Junction of Kansu and Battery streets, Yau Ma Tei, Kowloon;

101

daily 10am–3.30pm; MTR: Jordan; map p.134 B4

A mecca for collectors from all over the world, Hong Kong's Jade Market is a wonderful place to spend a morning browsing and soaking up the atmosphere. According to Chinese belief, jade wards off evil spirits and protects travellers, and you will find everything from rare and valuable jade carvings to small, inexpensive trinkets. Do not invest in expensive jade, though, unless you have an expert on hand.

Ladies' Market

Tung Choi Street, Mong Kok, Kowloon; daily 12.30–10.30pm; MTR: Mong Kok (exit E2); map p.132 B3

While it sells many other things as well as those specifically for women, the Ladies' Market is especially good for bags, accessories and inexpensive women's clothing. It is more manageable than Temple Street, so it is worth popping in here late afternoon before tackling the nearby Night Market.

Spring Garden Lane Market

Spring Garden Lane, between

Shipping it Home

Many larger stores will help with the packaging and shipment of purchases and can offer advice about insurance policies to cover fragile items. These can be bought at most of the bigger stores as a simple add-on to purchases. Many of the larger hotels can also organise a mailing service, and Hong Kong's post offices cater well for shoppers, with a range of on-site packaging materials available. Staff can offer advice and relevant documents for land and sea shipments. Postage rates are reasonable, and the service is very reliable.

Queen's Road East and Johnston Road, Wan Chai; daily 9am–10pm; MTR: Wan Chai; map p.139 A2

Some real rock-bottom bargains and a good starting point to explore Wan Chai's nearby street market.

Stanley Market

Stanley Village Road, Stanley, Southside; daily 11am–6pm; bus: 6, 6A, 6X or 260 from Central

The historic lanes of Stanley are jam-packed with vendors selling Chinese artwork, silk collectables, curios and factory overruns. Locals and visitors flock here for its relaxed seaside atmosphere and restaurants.

Temple Street Night Market

Temple Street, Yau Ma Tei, Kowloon; daily 2–10pm; MTR: Jordan (exit A); map p.132 B1

Awash with rows of brightly lit stalls hawking an astonishing variety of clothing, pens,

Opposite: flowers and fish have their own markets.

watches, DVDs, electronic gadgets, hardware and luggage, the Night Market is ordered chaos in action. Busy food stalls do a roaring trade in fresh seafood and hotpot dishes, and fortune-tellers and Chinese Opera enthusiasts cluster at the Yau Ma Tei end of the street. It does not really get going until after sunset.

Western Market
323 Des Voeux Road, Sheung Wan, Western; daily 10am–7pm; MTR: Sheung Wan; map p.136 B4
Sheung Wan's main market is a handsomely renovated Edwardian building filled with Chinese handicraft stores and fabric shops.

Yuen Po Street Bird Garden Market
Yuen Po Street, Mong Kok, Kowloon; daily 7am–8pm; MTR: Prince Edward (exit B1); map p.132 C4
You will hear the warble of the Bird Garden, on one side of the Flower Market (see p.101), before you see it. This charming Chinese-style garden is the favourite gathering place for Hong Kong's songbird owners, and the street and garden contain some 70 songbird stalls as well as courtyards and 'moon' gates. The market sells everything from intricately crafted cages (which make good souvenirs) to nutritious grasshoppers. Birds are priced according to their singing ability.

Factory Outlets, Seconds and Wholesale

As well as markets, other Hong Kong trademarks are the scores of places that, for a fraction of the prices you

Right: colourful goods and characters at the Jade Market.

would probably pay back home, sell samples, overruns and slightly damaged seconds of locally made clothes originally intended for export.

As a rule of thumb, bargain-priced womenswear, menswear, T-shirts and jeans, trainers and other footwear and children's clothes can be found in the **factory outlets** along **Spring Garden Lane Market** and **Johnston Road** in Wan Chai; **Jardine's Crescent** and **Lee Garden Road** in Causeway Bay; at **Stanley Market**; in Kowloon, along **Haiphong** and **Granville** roads in Tsim Sha Tsui; and around the **Ladies' Market** and **Fa Yuen Street** in Mong Kok. **Temple Street Night Market** in Yau Ma Tei, Kowloon, has cheap menswear.

Horizon Plaza (2 Wing Lee Street, Ap Lei Chau, Aberdeen; bus: 70, 98, 590) has at least a dozen designer outlets and a Lane Crawford Warehouse (25/F). It's a must if you are looking for bargain furniture to ship home. It houses both furniture and fashion outlets: **Tequila Kola** (1/F) is worth the sidetrack for contemporary Asian furniture; **Shambala** (2/F) has vintage and repro Asian finds.

Milan Station
26 Wellington Street, Central; tel: 2736 3388; www.milanstation. com.hk; daily noon–10pm; MTR: Central; map p.136 C3
A local chain that stocks all kinds of (authentic) second-hand designer bags in mint condition. Branches in Percival Street, Causeway Bay, and around the city.

103

Above: Temple Street Night Market *(see p.102)*.

Sasa

G/F, World Trade Centre, 280 Gloucester Road, Causeway Bay; tel: 2805 6838; www.sasa. com; daily 11am–10pm; MTR: Causeway Bay; map p.139 D3

One of the cheapest cosmetics shops around, with vast ranges of local and international brands, many imported direct from the manufacturer, but the most exciting thing is the super-low prices for just-launched luxury-brand perfumes. Branches all around Hong Kong.

Shopping For...

ART, ANTIQUES, FURNITURE AND ASIAN HANDICRAFTS

Hong Kong is a thriving centre for arts and crafts from the whole of Asia as well as China, with museum-quality antique furniture, ceramics, sculptures, textiles and traditional paintings from Tibet, Japan and Southeast Asia. More affordable are modern Chinese or Vietnamese paintings, rugs, reproduction Korean chests and antique Chinese furniture or ceramics, Thai Buddha figurines, Bali-

nese woodwork and Chinese folk paintings. For shops that deal specifically in Chinese art, craftwork, clothing and so on, *see under* **Chinese Fashion, Arts and Crafts**, *p.105*.

The greatest concentrations of antique dealers are around **Hollywood Road** in Sheung Wan, where **Upper Lascar Row**, also known as **Cat Street Bazaar**, is always good for browsing.

There are also a number of top-quality antiques dealers in malls, such as **Pacific Place** in Admiralty and at **Harbour City** and **New World Centre** on Kowloonside. For more competitive prices on Chinese and Asian antiques and contemporary clothes, furnishings and design items, check out too the wholesale import/export

outlets in **Aberdeen** (bus: 70, 98, 590). They are conveniently concentrated in two big warehouse-style buildings: the **Hing Wai Centre**, 7 Tin Wan Praya Road, and **Horizon Plaza** *(see p.103)*.

Fine art galleries are also concentrated in Central, **SoHo**, and Sheung Wan. Check under exhibition listings in the local newspapers, or in the free *HKTB Hong Kong Diary, Where* or *HK* magazines.

Alan Chan Creations

Shop BL5A, B/F, Peninsula Hotel, Salisbury Road, Kowloon; www.alanchancreations.com; daily 9.30am–7pm; MTR: Tsim Sha Tsui; map p. 134 C1

Stylishly nostalgic graphic design items by one of Hong Kong's leading design gurus.

Amazing Grace Elephant Company

Star House, Salisbury Road, Tsim Sha Tsui, Kowloon; tel: 2730 5455; www.amazing gracehk.com; daily 9am–9.30pm; MTR: Tsim Sha Tsui; map p.134 B1

Lively store with sarongs, batiks, jewellery, carvings and so on from across Asia as well as China. Also has a shop at the airport.

Hong Kong Museum of Art

10 Salisbury Road, Tsim Sha Tsui, Kowloon; tel: 2721 0116;

Below: Bird Garden Market *(see p.103)*.

Above: antiques and abaci.

Fri and Sun–Wed 10am–6pm, Sat 10am–8pm; MTR: Tsim Sha Tsui; map p.134 C1
The museum's gift shop is a fine place to pick up smaller gift items and cards.

Indigo Living
Horizon Plaza, 2 Lee Wing Street, Ap Lei Chau; tel: 2555 0540; Mon–Sat 10am–6pm, Sun noon–6pm; bus: 671
Interior furnishings, accessories with a sophisticated Asian twist. Also Indigo Kids range. Branches in Central and Repulse Bay.

Mountain Folkcraft
12 Wo On Lane, off D'Aguilar Street, Central; tel: 2525 3199; Mon–Sat 9.30am–6.30pm; MTR: Central, then Mid-Levels Escalator; map p.137 C3
Enduring shop with unusual items and unique fabrics mostly from China and Tibet.

OVO
16 Queen's Road East, Wan Chai; tel: 2526 7226; www.ovohome. com.hk; Mon–Sat 10.30am–7.30pm, Sun 2–7.30pm; MTR: Wan Chai; map p.138 A2
Modern shop filled with sleek, high-quality custom-made furniture.

CHINESE FASHION, ARTS AND CRAFTS
For the Rolls-Royce of things Chinese, do not miss the designer-chic **Shanghai Tang**. You can also pick up cheaper *cheongsams* and other Chinese garments in the Lanes (**Li Yuen Streets East** and **West**) and in the scores of boutiques on the roads that lead off **Nathan Road** in Tsim Sha Tsui, towards TST East.

Buyer Beware
Though there is nothing it cannot buy in Hong Kong, it has ceased to be the guaranteed 'amazing bargain' it once was for electronics products. Be wary of tricksters who sell fake peripherals and so on in apparently original, branded packaging, and try to avoid buying anything that does not have an international guarantee. Do not be fooled by signs advertising that a shop has 'Tax Free' prices either: Hong Kong is a free port, so all of the city's shops enjoy tax-free status. Look out for the Hong Kong Tourism Board's black-and-gold 'QTS' (Quality Tourism Services) scheme logo on shop doors or windows, or visit the website (www.discoverhongkong.com/qts) for a list of accredited shops and restaurants. Especially useful when buying jewellery, watches and electronics, it indicates retailers accredited by the tourism board for quality in goods and service.

Markets are also a good bet for Chinese clothes and accessories. The **Ladies' Market** *(see p.102)* stocks a wide selection of dresses and handbags, and **Stanley Market** *(see p.102)* sells everything from a complete mandarin suit for a baby to exquisite *cheongsams* for five-year-olds, and far, far cheaper (but good-quality) versions of the silk scarves sold in Shanghai Tang.

G.O.D
Leighton Centre, 77 Leighton Road, Entrance on Sharp Street, Causeway Bay; tel: 2890 5555; www.god.com.hk; daily noon–10pm; MTR: Causeway Bay; map p.139 C2
An imaginative and humorous take on Chinese crafts and other local products. Homegrown G.O.D (pronounced 'gee-oh-dee', a phonetic play on the Cantonese for 'live better') is a browser's playground stuffed with affordable funky homewares, unusual clothing and quirky Asian knick-knacks. There is plenty of local humour in its range of unique bags, which feature among other things images of housing estates and a play on the blue, red and white *amah* bags. Other branches are in Central and Tsim Sha Tsui.

Above: Mao memorabilia for sale at Cat Street.

Hong Kong Design Gallery

Level 1, Hong Kong Convention and Exhibition Centre, 1 Harbour Road, Wan Chai; tel: 2584 4146; www.hkdesigngallery.tdctrade. com; Mon–Fri 10am–7.30pm, Sat 10am–7pm, Sun noon–7.30pm; MTR: Wan Chai; map p.138 A3

Inspiring new jewellery, accessories, household design, gadgets and more by up-and-coming Hong Kong designers, in an official showcase gallery.

Shanghai Tang

1 Duddell Street, Central; tel: 2525 7333; www.shanghai tang.com; daily 10.30am–8pm; MTR: Central; map p.137 C3

The four-storey mansion on Duddell Street is the flagship for the Shanghai Tang brand that excels in mixing contemporary Chinese design with retro fashions in lush fabrics. An expert made-to-measure service is offered. Gift items include novelty watches with tiny dim sum servings instead of numbers, and Chairman Mao cufflinks. Branches in

Pacific Place, Elements, 1881 Heritage, and the airport.

ELECTRONICS, COMPUTERS AND PHOTOGRAPHIC

If you are prepared to shop around, you can still find very competitive prices on electronic goods here. Shops selling digital cameras, DVD players, music systems, computers and all kinds of other gadgets cluster mainly in **Causeway Bay** and, above all, **Tsim Sha Tsui**, Kowloon, especially along **Nathan**, **Peking**, **Mody** and **Carnarvon** roads. As in tourist hotspots around the world, you need to keep an eye out for unscrupulous shopkeepers. Compare prices, resist pressure-sales tactics and always check the goods and receipt before leaving the shop. If in doubt, stick to traders bearing the HKTB's official **QTS** (Quality Tourism Services) logo. If you are not comfortable with the haggling process, the

fixed-price chains **Broadway** or **Fortress** are good alternatives.

In the small shops that make up the 'computer malls', be prepared for sometimes very pushy (but sometimes also helpful) service. A wide range of hard- and software is available, and you will shave a little, if not a great deal, off home prices. What you will find is a vastly extended variety of peripherals, from games, specialist programmes, novelty add-ons, plenty to tempt you.

Computers and peripherals sold here have overwhelmingly been made, naturally, for the Asian market. Always check the keyboard before you leave the shop – some come with Chinese characters only. Check too that all modem or other ports are compatible with those in your home country.

298 Computer Zone

298 Hennessy Road, Wan Chai; daily, shop times vary; MTR: Wan Chai; map p.139 C3

A labyrinth of tiny stores over three floors. Prices can be rock-bottom, but this can be because some of the goods are pirated or poor-quality non-branded copies. You need to know what you are doing.

Broadway

Shop 714–715, Times Square, 1 Matheson Street, Causeway Bay; tel: 2506 1330; www.broadway. com.hk; daily 11am–10pm; MTR: Causeway Bay; map p.139 C3

Broadway has every kind of electronic and camera product displayed in user-friendly fashion, and are also official Apple resellers. Several branches around Hong Kong.

Computer Mall, 10/F Windsor House

311 Gloucester Road, corner of Great George Street, Causeway Bay; tel: 2895 0668;

www.windsorhouse.hk; daily 10am–10pm; MTR: Causeway Bay; map p.139 D3

One floor of shops with every kind of computer and peripherals imaginable.

Fortress

Shops 718–719, Times Square, 1 Matheson Street, Causeway Bay; tel: 2506 0031; www.fortress. com.hk; Mon–Fri 11am–10pm, Sat–Sun 10.30am–10pm; MTR: Causeway Bay; map p.139 C3

Cameras, audio, computers and more. Over 30 branches.

Golden Shopping Centre

146–152 Fuk Wa Street, Sham Shui Po, Kowloon; daily, shop times vary; MTR: Sham Shui Po

HK's original electronics mall, with ultra-low prices, for computer parts and peripherals, plus lots of non-branded electronics, parallel imports and the occasional fake phone, non-branded or pirated goods.

Mongkok Computer Centre

8 Nelson Street, Mong Kok, Kowloon; tel: 2302 0858; daily, shop times vary; MTR: Mong Kok; map p.132 C3

Three floors of every computer product you can think of.

Photo Scientific Appliances

6 Stanley Street, Central; tel: 2522 1903; Mon–Sat 9am–7pm; MTR: Central; map p.136 C3

Many local professional photographers buy their equipment at this superior store.

Star Computer City

Star House, Salisbury Road, Tsim Sha Tsui, Kowloon; daily, shop times vary; MTR: Tsim Sha Tsui; map p.134 B1

Another computer mall, with lots of tiny shops.

FASHION AND DESIGNER SHOPPING

All the fashion heavyweights have been in Hong Kong for years, but this has not stopped a spate of high-profile launches and relaunches, often coinciding with the revamping or opening of major malls. This is particularly so in the Central district, where the stylish triumvirate of **The Landmark** (see p.100), neighbouring **Prince's Building** (see p.100) and the stylish new **Chater House** (Chater Road) fly the flag for the world's designer fashion fraternity.

Superbrands **Louis Vuitton** and **Gucci** have both opened architecturally striking flagship stores in the **Landmark** (see p.100). Vuitton, with its fourth 'global concept' store, occupies three floors and is fronted by an enormous trunk-shaped hoarding featuring the famous cherry monogram. This has set the scene for the arrival of a glut of upmarket brands, which attract the fashion cognoscenti like bees to honey. First came a mini version of the UK's **Harvey Nichols**, to be joined by another Brit, **Paul Smith**, and the über-trendy Japanese label **A Bathing Ape**. When **Abercrombie & Fitch** took over four floors in the Pedder Building in 2012, the rent was said to hit US$1 million a month.

These stop-the-traffic flagships are upstaged only by the veritable empire created by **Armani**, a few hundred metres away in the Chater Building.

Further on towards the harbour, labels from **agnès b** (who has opened her first and only travel concept store in Hong Kong) to local designer **Vivienne Tam** can be found in the **IFC Mall** (see p.100), where it is worth calling into the city's largest **Lane Crawford** (see p.101) store for a seat at the trendy CD Bar. At the in-store Martini Bar flagging shoppers can relax with a cocktail while engulfed in Bose surround-sound and check their stock and shares on the Hang Seng index.

More labels abound at **Pacific Place** and **Times Square** (see p.100, 101) in Causeway Bay, in the arcades in many top-flight hotels, and in the **New World Centre** and **Harbour City** (see p.100) complexes and on **Canton Road** in Tsim Sha Tsui, Kowloon. Low- to mid-range fashion chains have outlets in virtually every shopping district in Hong Kong, with top international brand names competing with locally produced labels such as Bossini, U2, Giordano and Episode.

Aside from Vivienne Tam, other home-grown designer

Below: Stanley Market.

talent to look out for includes Lu Lu Cheung, Allan Chiu, Barney Cheng and Walter Ma. And do not miss **Island Beverley** mall in Causeway Bay *(see p.100)*, for an innovative crop of young designers.

Not to be ignored is another aspect of Hong Kong shopping: its many factory outlets and discount houses. For these, *see p.103*.

A Bathing Ape

G/F, 10 Queen's Road Central, Central; tel: 2868 9448; www.bape.com; daily 11am–8pm; MTR: Central; map p.137 C3

Also known just as BAPE, this cult Japanese youth label is easily picked out by its big gorilla logo above the shop's entrance, opposite the Landmark, and by the queues that snake around the building on new-line delivery days.

Giorgio Armani

Chater House, 11 Chater Road, Central; tel: 2532 7700; www.armani.com; daily 10am–7.30pm; MTR: Central; map p.137 D3

An Armani fiefdom has been created in the Chater Building, catering for every need: as well as the fashion lines for women, men and kids, the portfolio includes *Armani Fiori*, *Armani Casa* and *Armani Dolci*. When you have done shopping, there is the Armani Winebar and Lounge, a world

first for anyone wishing to eat and drink a brand as well as wear it. There are also Armani stores in most big malls.

Joyce Boutique

Shop 232 Pacific Place, 88 Queensway, Admiralty; tel: 2523 5944; daily 10.30am–7.30pm; www.joyce.com; MTR: Admiralty; map p.137 E2

Joyce Ma's elegant stores have been among Hong Kong's foremost showcases for international fashion – especially European and Japanese labels – for over 20 years: upmarket, stylish and prestigious. Branches include 16 Queen's Road, Central, 106 Canton Road, Tsim Sha Tsui, and the Joyce Warehouse discount house in Aberdeen.

JEWELLERY, WATCHES AND GEMSTONES

Hong Kong has the world's largest jade market, the third largest diamond trading centre after New York and Antwerp, and one of the largest gold brokers. It is also a centre for trading in precious stones from all over Asia. Many finished jewellery items, from simple gold bangles to intricately designed diamond necklaces, are manufactured in Hong Kong.

Gold and jewellery factory outlets abound in **Hung Hom**

in Kowloon, but prices here have risen steeply over the past few years. Better bargains can be had in the shops along **Queen's Road Central**. Top-flight hotel shopping arcades are another place to find quality jewellers, and there is a big choice on **Yee Wo Street** and **Hennessy Road** in Causeway Bay, and along **Nathan Road** in Tsim Sha Tsui.

For a professional gemmologist to certify authenticity before you buy diamonds, jade or gems, call the **Gemmological Association of Hong Kong** (tel: 2366 6006).

Larry Jewelry

Pacific Place Centre, 88 Queensway; tel: 2868 3993; www.larryjewelry.com; Mon–Sat 11am–7.30pm, Sun 11am–7pm; MTR: Admiralty; map p.137 E2

One of Hong Kong's finest jewellers, with three more branches.

OPTICAL SERVICES

Hong Kong is a great place to buy eye-wear, whether it is prescription lenses or the latest designer sunglasses. Frames and contact lenses are bang up to date and excellent value; eye tests are free, and the service quick and efficient. There are hundreds of small opticians, as well as the major chains.

Below: Temple Street Night Market *(see p.102)*.

Above: designer shops are easily found.

Bunn's Divers
188 Johnston Road, Wan Chai; tel: 3422 3322; www.bunns divers.com; hours vary, call ahead for details; MTR: Wan Chai; map p.138 B2
A specialist diving shop that stocks prescription goggles and diving masks.

Fox Optical
12 Cochrane Street, Central; tel: 2541 3018; daily 10am–7pm; MTR: Central; map p.136 C3
A good-quality independent optician. Recommended.

Lenscrafters
G/F, 56 Queen's Road Central, Central; tel: 2840 0621; daily 10am–7.30pm; MTR: Central; map p.137 C3
Another reliable large-scale chain optician, with branches all over Hong Kong and the New Territories.

Mandarin Optical
79 Queen's Road Central, Central; daily 10am–7pm; MTR: Central; map p.136 C3
Also a lens manufacturer, so service is especially fast.

Optical 88
65 Percival Street, Causeway Bay; tel: 2891 7316, www. optical88.com; daily 11am–10pm; MTR: Causeway Bay; map p.139 C3
Largest of all Hong Kong's retail opticians, with scores of efficient outlets all around the Territory.

TAILORING
Hong Kong tailors are justifiably renowned for their skills, both in classic tailoring and in copying existing garments. Prices naturally vary according to the work involved, and the quality and quantity of cloth and trimmings, but you can get a good custom-tailored shirt from HK$250, or a man's or woman's suit from HK$2,500 and up.

Quality tailors usually require that you allow time for a couple of fittings; there are exceptions, but in general the days of the so-called 24-hour suit, at on-the-floor prices, are gone. Look for the Hong Kong Tourism Board's QTS logo when choosing a tailor. Remember too that Hong Kong cobblers can also make custom-made shoes to complete your outfit.

Pursue
2/F, 13 Lan Kwai Fong, Central; tel: 2537 0993; www.pursue hk.com; Mon–Sat noon–9pm; MTR: Central; map p.137 C2
For something different, try this modern store. Catering to men and women, it also has a lounge and bar area complete with entertainment system.

Sam's Tailor
G/F, Burlington Arcade K, 94 Nathan Road, Tsim Sha Tsui, Kowloon; tel: 2367 9423; www.samstailor.com; Mon–Sat 10am–7.30pm, Sun 10am–12.30am; MTR: Tsim Sha Tsui; map p.134 C2
Most famous of Hong Kong tailors, clothing celebrities from the Prince of Wales to Rod Stewart. Nevertheless, it is still a modest little shop, and all customers are expertly and courteously catered for, at all kinds of prices.

Soong Salon de Mode
2/F, Flat A, Hangchung Mansions, 8–10 Hankow Road, Kowloon; tel: 2366 0480; daily 10am–7pm; MTR: Tsim Sha Tsui; map p.134 B2
Expat girls flock here for glamorous new creations and copies.

Tailor Kwan
Escalator Link Alley, 2/F, Central Market, Central; http://tailor kwan.com; daily 10am–7pm; MTR: Central; map p.136 C3

William Cheng & Son
8/F, 38 Hankow Road, Tsim Sha Tsui, Kowloon; tel: 2739 7888; daily 10am–7pm; MTR: Tsim Sha Tsui; map p.134 B2

Yuen's Tailors
Escalator Link Alley, 2/F, Central Market, Central; tel: 2854 9649; daily 10.30am–7.30pm; MTR: Central; map p.136 C3
Suits, shirts and tuxedos made by Hong Kong's favourite kilt maker.

Sport

Despite its relatively small population, Hong Kong packs a wealth of sport and activities into its territory, with options ranging from hiking and golf to rugby, tennis and horse racing. While events like the annual Dragon Boat championships are typical Hong Kong experiences, the sporting calendar is also packed with high-profile competitions in international sports that attract world-class sportsmen and women. With online booking to smooth the way, keeping up with your favourite kind of exercise and maybe seeing a major sporting event during your visit could not be easier.

Cricket

Great pitch action can be enjoyed at the annual Hong Kong Cricket Sixes at Kowloon Cricket Club in late October, early November. Sanctioned by the ICC its the sport's longest-running, best-established and most high-profile sixes tournament with teams competing in an action-packed, six-a-side format. Events aside, the Hong Kong Cricket Association website has details of all Hong Kong's clubs and the season's matches.

Hong Kong Cricket Association
Tel: 2504 8102;
www.cricket.com.hk

Cycling

You would be very brave to take to Hong Kong's urban roads on a bike, but cyclists will find cycling paths in the New Territories, particularly around Tolo Harbour, in the northeast beyond Sha Tin. Visitors can rent bikes in Sha Tin or Tai Po. Elsewhere, bikes can be rented in Shek O on Hong Kong Island, and on Cheung Chau, Lamma and especially Lantau islands. Bikes are in big demand at weekends – book, or hire early – and paths are very busy.

Not all trails in Hong Kong's country parks are open for mountain biking (check the signs), but a handful of parks do have trails; for details, contact the HKMBA.

Hong Kong Cycling Association
Tel: 2504 8176;
www.cycling.org.hk
Mainly involved in competition cycling, with an annual race calendar.

Hong Kong Mountain Biking Association
www.hkmba.org
Essential source of information, particularly on authorised routes in country parks, maps and other facilities.

Dragon Boat Racing

Dragon boat races are held throughout June, in the Dragon Boat Festival *(Tuen Ng)*. Steeped in tradition – it commemorates a 3rd-century BC Chinese hero

Left: golfing with a view.

Left: Happy Valley racecourse.

Sport of Kings

You do not have to have any affinity with the racehorses to imbibe the night-time buzz at Happy Valley racecourse. The evening is as much about Hong Kong's unique tightly stacked cityscape and vertiginous tower blocks twinkling down over the packed stands as it is about thundering hooves. If you are a racing fan, though, do not miss the prestige international races such as the lucrative Hong Kong Derby (Mar), Queen Elizabeth II Cup (Apr) and Hong Kong International Races (Dec), when world-class horses and jockeys fly in to compete for the world's richest purses. All are held at the Sha Tin track. Race meetings are held every Wednesday night at Happy Valley, and every Saturday and Sunday at Sha Tin, from September to June. Alternatively, get a stylish introduction to Hong Kong racing with the HKTB's Come Horseracing Tour, which gives a day's racing at Sha Tin or an evening at Happy Valley in the comfort of the hallowed Hong Kong Jockey Club Members' Enclosure.

who threw himself into a river rather than bow to the orders of a tyrannical ruler – this is one of Hong Kong's most colourful sports.

The **Hong Kong International Dragon Boat Races**, the main competitive event, with teams from many countries as well as Hong Kong, are held over two days towards the end of June, but there are local races throughout the month, and for weeks before the festival it is possible to catch crews in training before the big event. You can catch the action at various locations around Hong Kong including Aberdeen, Stanley, Sha Tin, Tai Po, Cheung Chau and Lantau Island; for each year's calendar, check www.discoverhongkong.com.
SEE ALSO FESTIVALS, P.41

Football

Hong Kong only has an amateur football (soccer) league, but even so Hong Kongers are crazy about football, above all the English Premiership, which is shown in all the city's sports bars.

Hunger for live football is slaked mainly by two tournaments, the Lunar New Year Cup, which pits the Chinese national side and/or a Hong Kong team against a mixed bag of other national teams around the time of Chinese New Year, and the Barclays Asia Trophy in late July, when English Premiership clubs get some pre-season training (Liverpool, Chelsea and Newcastle have all taken part in different years) against teams from mainland China and the rest of Asia. Games are played at the Hong Kong Stadium. For more information, see www.hkfa.com/en.

Hong Kong Stadium

55 Eastern Hospital Road, So Kon Po, near Causeway Bay; tel: 2895 7926; www.lcsd.gov.hk/stadium; bus: 2, 5, 19, 25; map p.139 E1

Hong Kong's largest sports venue, seating 40,000, hosts a range of football competitions and the annual rugby sevens tournament.

Golf

Hong Kong has only one public golf course, the

Jockey Club Kau Sai Chau public golf course (Mon, Wed–Thur 7am–8pm, Tue 11am–8pm, Fri–Sun 7am–10pm). Set among rolling hills on Kau Sai Chau Island, and affords stunning views of the South China Sea, Sai Kung hills and nearby islands. Gary Player designed two of its three courses.

Non-members are welcome from Monday to Friday at the Hong Kong Golf Club's two courses at Deep Water Bay and Fanling.

A must-see for golf fans is the four-day **Hong Kong**

Open, each November at the Hong Kong Golf Club in Fanling. For details see www.ubshongkongopen.com.

Hong Kong Golf Club
www.hkgolfclub.org
Jockey Club Kau Sai Chau
www.kscgolf.org.hk

Horse Racing

No one loves a wager like the Chinese, but the only places gambling is actually legal in the SAR are the Hong Kong Jockey Club's two racetracks and their network of betting shops. The racing season is the perfect marriage between the British affection for 'race day' and the Chinese obsession with numbers and fortune. It is not every day you get to bet on such auspicious horses as *Ambitious Dragon, Tiger Storm* or *Hero of Abalone.*

The **Happy Valley** and **Sha Tin** racecourses are home to some of the richest races in the world (and Sha Tin's video screen is also one of the world's biggest). Entry to the stands costs from HK$10, which is also the cost of a minimum bet. Races are held every week from September to June, every Wednesday night at Happy Valley (usually beginning at 7.15pm), and on Saturdays and Sundays at Sha Tin (usually from 1–6pm). Check out the **Hong Kong Jockey Club** website (www.hkjc.com) for a full race calendar and all the latest information.

Happy Valley Racecourse
Happy Valley Stand, Happy Valley; tel: 2895 1523; www.hkjc.com; bus/tram: Happy Valley; map p.138 C1
Also home to the Hong Kong Racing Museum.

To see the truly wild side of Hong Kong, contact **Kayak-and-Hike** (tel: 9300 5197; www.kayak-and-hike.com). Run by long-term HK resident Paul Etherington, this agency offers a wide range of adventure trips – many by kayak – hikes and climbs, above all into the wild Sai Kung Country Park in the eastern New Territories.

SEE ALSO MUSEUMS AND GALLERIES, P.66
Sha Tin Racecourse
Sha Tin, New Territories; tel: 2696 6223; www.hkjc.com; MTR: Sha Tin Racecourse

Rugby

The Hong Kong Rugby Sevens is one of Hong Kong's most popular annual events, and you do not have to be a rugby fan to enjoy it. The Sevens is basically one long fever-pitched party, held over three days in late March at the Hong Kong Stadium *(see p.111)*. Twenty-four seven-a-side teams compete to win the coveted Hong Kong Sevens championship, and, with the exception of the 20-minute cup final, each match lasts just 14 minutes. The atmosphere in the stands is electric. Tickets sell out quickly, so book in advance (www.hksevens.com). Look out for restaurant and entertainment outlets displaying the rugby sevens offers: visitors just need to show a travel document to benefit.

Swimming

Public swimming pools are a godsend when Hong Kong's humidity kicks in. The sports complex in Kowloon Park incorporates an Olympic-

Left: waterskiing and sand castles.

sized indoor and an outdoor pool, and there are smaller outdoor pools in Victoria Park (closed November to March). For a full list of public pools, see www.lcsd.gov.hk. Many hotels have good-sized pools too.

Then there are the beaches. About 41 of Hong Kong's shark-netted beaches have lifeguards, along with facilities including changing rooms, showers, swimming rafts and refreshments kiosks (from April to October). Popular swimming beaches include **Repulse Bay** and **Cheung Sha** beach on Lantau Island.

Above: keeping the beaches safe.

Kowloon Park
Kowloon Park Drive, Tsim Sha Tsui, Kowloon; MTR: Tsim Sha Tsui, Jordan; map p.134 B2

Victoria Park
Between Victoria Park Road and Causeway Road, Causeway Bay; MTR: Causeway Bay, Tin Hau; map p.139 E4

Tennis
Public tennis courts can be found in Victoria Park and Kowloon Park. Some hotels also have courts, and can sometimes book spots for guests at private clubs.

In terms of competitions Victoria Park also has a well-equipped tennis stadium with a seating capacity of 3,611, which has hosted a number of international tournaments including the Davis Cup and the Champions Challenge, a premier women's tour tournament, held every January.

Victoria Park Tennis Stadium
Between Victoria Park Road and Causeway Road, Causeway Bay; MTR: Causeway Bay, Tin Hau
SEE ALSO PARKS AND GARDENS, P.85

Walking and Hiking
Hong Kong's 23 country parks offer endless opportunities for walking and hiking, and this is one of the most popular weekend pastimes. Significant trails include the 50km (30-mile) Hong Kong Trail that spans all of Hong Kong Island's five country parks, and the 70km (40-mile) Lantau Trail on Lantau Island.

Former governor and keen walker Sir Murray MacLehose opened up large tracts of local countryside to trekkers, and the famous 62km (38-mile) **MacLehose Trail** spans the New Territories. Shorter trails such as the various **Peak** trails and the cross-island trail on **Lamma** abound. Keen walkers should pick up a copy of *The Inside Guide to Hikes and Walks in Hong Kong*, available free from HKTB Visitor Information Centres. SEE ALSO WALKS AND VIEWS, P.126, 129

Windsurfing
Windsurfing won Hong Kong its first Olympic gold medal in 1996, and the sport has steadily grown in popularity. Medallist Lee Lai-Shan trained off Cheung Chau Island, which has become a popular spot for windsurfers. Boards are available for hire at Kwun Yam Beach on Cheung Chau, as well as in Stanley and a number of other locations.

Check out the website www.windsurfing.org.hk for more details.

Marathon Running
The Hong Kong Marathon is Hong Kong's biggest outdoor sporting event by number of participants. Held in late February or early March, it attracts around 40,000 runners, including many of the world's best. The event includes a half marathon and a 10km (6-mile) run as well as a full marathon, on a course that runs past some of Hong Kong's most dramatic scenery. The marathon course starts on Nathan Road in Tsim Sha Tsui, runs up to Tsing Yi Island and along the Tsing Ma Bridge then turns back south to finish in Victoria Park on Hong Kong Island.

Temples and Historic Sites

Hong Kong may feel new, but it has been inhabited for millennia, first by the *Tanka* boat dwellers, followed by the Manchus and Hakkas, and more latterly by the British. Each stage in Hong Kong's chequered past has left behind the remnants of different beliefs and ways of life. From Taoist temples and giant Buddhas to walled villages and an Anglican church, there is certainly a complex background of culture, history and belief to unearth if you know where to look.

Hong Kong Island

Government House
Upper Albert Road, Central; MTR: Central; map p.137 C2
The former residence of Britain's colonial governors was begun in neoclassical style in 1851, but considerably altered by the Japanese during World War II. The lush gardens are open to the public a few times a year, particularly when the azaleas are in bloom in March; check with the Hong Kong Tourist Board *(see p.39)* for details.

Man Mo Temple
126 Hollywood Road, Sheung Wan, Western; tel: 2540 0350; daily 8am–6pm; free, donations welcome; MTR: Sheung Wan; map p.136 B3
Tourists regularly throng the atmospheric Man Mo, but this does not inhibit the temple's regular worshippers from filling it with clouds of smoke from joss sticks and incense spirals that dangle photogenically from the ceiling. Man is the god of civil servants and of literature, Mo is the god of martial arts and war. There are usually old men and women pottering around in the dark recesses of the temple, lighting incense sticks or laying out offerings.

Old Supreme Court – Legislative Council
Jackson Road, Central; check with tourist offices for visiting times; MTR: Central; map p.137 D3
Opened in 1912, the two-storey granite structure was built in grand neoclassical style. It was converted in 1985 to house the Legislative Council (LegCo), until it moved to its new location in Admiralty in 2011.

St John's Cathedral
4–8 Garden Road, Central; tel: 2523 4157; www.stjohns cathedral.org.hk; Mon–Fri 9am–5pm, Sat–Sun 9am–noon; free;

Below: a study in details.

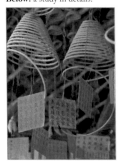

Left: Tian Tin Buddha at Po Lin Monastery *(see p.117)*.

lic Square Street, Yau Ma Tei, Kowloon; tel: 2332 9240; daily 7am–5pm; free, donations welcome; MTR: Yau Ma Tei; map p.132 B1

Over a century old, this temple complex is the main Tin Hau temple in Hong Kong city. The Taoist deity Tin Hau, goddess of the sea and protector of fisherfolk, has always been especially revered in Hong Kong, and there are scores of other temples to her throughout the Territory. Tin Hau's birthday in late April or May is a major festival, with colourful celebrations at all her temples, but especially in fishing villages around the coast.

Locals visit this city temple regularly, to leave offerings at an image of Tin Hau draped in intricately embroidered scarlet robes. To the right of the altar are 60 identi-

MTR: Central, then bus/tram: Queensway; map p.137 D2

Built in Victorian Gothic style in 1847–9, tranquil St John's is the oldest surviving Western religious building in Hong Kong, and the oldest Anglican church in East Asia.

Kowloon and New Kowloon

Chi Lin Nunnery

5 Chi Lin Drive, Diamond Hill, New Kowloon; tel: 2354 1730; daily 9am–4.30pm; free, donations welcome; MTR: Diamond Hill (exit C2)

Flanked by a lily pond and instantly recognisable by its beautifully embellished carved wooden roofs, the huge Buddhist Chi Lin complex was built between the 1930s and 1990s, but entirely in the classic style of the Tang dynasty (AD 618–907). Its seven wooden halls were even constructed using wooden tenons instead of nails. Nestled among the surrounding high-rise apartment blocks is the tranquil **Nan Lian Garden**, a relatively new public park also

built in the Tang style. The scenic garden is meticulously landscaped over an area of 3.5 hectares (8½ acres), in which every hill, rock, body of water, plant and timber structure has been placed according to specific rules and methods.

Former Kowloon-Canton Railway Clock Tower

By Star Ferry Pier, Tsim Sha Tsui, Kowloon; MTR: Tsim Sha Tsui; map p.134 B1

This clock tower came into operation in 1915, as part of the main station of the Kowloon-Canton Railway. The rest of the station was knocked down in 1978, but, unusually for Hong Kong, it was decided to keep the local landmark of the tower.

Hong Kong Observatory

134 Nathan Road, Tsim Sha Tsui, Kowloon; tel: 2926 8200; MTR: Tsim Sha Tsui; map p.134 C3

Built in 1883, the Observatory sits on a small hill amid a pretty garden, and continues to monitor Hong Kong's weather.

Tin Hau Temple

Corner of Nathan Road and Pub-

Monumental Hong Kong

Hectic Hong Kong does not give the impression of caring too much for its heritage, but it is surprising to find how much remains of 5,000 years of human settlement in the Territory, and it is a little-known fact that it has 86 officially declared monuments. They include stone carvings that date back thousands of years, venerable Taoist temples, walled villages that still house living communities, and remnants of Hong Kong's colonial history, such as forts and even lighthouses. The handsome granite Western Market, the former Wan Chai Post Office (oldest surviving one in Hong Kong), the former Kowloon British School and St John's Cathedral all bear the hallmarks of British heritage.

Left: divination sticks and incense.

Liu Man Shek Tong Ancestral Hall

Man Hau Tsuen, near Sheung Shui; Wed–Sun 9am–1pm, 2–5pm; free; MTR: East line to Sheung Shui

The key attraction of Sheung Shui, the last town before the main crossing into mainland China, is this finely preserved hall, built in 1751 by the Liu clan as a meeting place and to honour their ancestors.

Man Lun Fung Ancestral Hall and Tai Fu Tai Mansion

San Tin, between Yuen Long and Sheung Shui; daily 9am–1pm, 2–5pm; free; MTR: West line to Yuen Long, then bus: 75, 76, 76K

Around the village of San Tin are the **Ancestral Hall**, smaller than the Liu Man Shek, and thought to have been erected at the end of the 17th century in honour of a leading member of the Man clan, and **Tai Fu Tai Mansion**, a stately residence built in 1865 by a senior Man clan member who was bestowed the title of *Tai Fu* (mandarin) by the Qing emperor. It is the best-

cal deities, which represent every year of the 60-year lunar calendar. Worshippers place 'Hell Bank' notes under the god dedicated to the years of their birth. The adjoining square has a very Chinese atmosphere, with elderly locals playing Chinese chess and chewing the fat.

Wong Tai Sin Temple

Wong Tai Sin Road, Wong Tai Sin, New Kowloon; tel: 2327 8141; www.siksikyuen.org.hk; daily 7am–5.30pm; free, entrance charge to some areas, donations welcome; MTR: Wong Tai Sin

You will know you have arrived at the Wong Tai Sin temple when you hear the sound of rattling *chim*, the bamboo fortune sticks used for fortune-telling. Known as 'the fortune-tellers' temple', this Taoist temple complex in a natural setting at the heart of urban Kowloon is probably the liveliest and most colourful place of worship in the whole of Hong Kong. It is certainly one of the most rewarding for outsiders to visit, constantly bustling with worshippers. The rear of the main altar is carved to show the story of the god Wong Tai Sin, a sim-

ple shepherd who is said to have been given the formula for an elixir for immortality by a heavenly spirit. There is a small entrance charge to some areas, such as the lovely **Good Wish Garden**, which may also be closed at some times.

New Territories

Kam Tin Walled Villages

Kam Tin, near Yuen Long; MTR: West line to Kam Sheung Road

Around the town of Kam Tim in the northwest of the Territories are two walled villages: **Kat Hing Wai** is the grandest of the remaining such villages in Hong Kong, a moated settlement built around 1600, and still lived in by the Hakka people. **Shui Tau Tsuen**, further from Kam Tin, is smaller, but has well-restored temples.

Kun Lung Gate Tower

San Wai, near Fanling; MTR: East line to Fanling

Serving as the entrance to San Wai, a small, wonderfully preserved village of the Tang clan, this tower was built in 1744. It is the best surviving gate tower of a walled village in the New Territories.

As part of its tour programme, the Hong Kong Tourism Board (HKTB) offers a convenient five-hour slice of Hong Kong's traditions – as well as a glimpse of the New Territories – on its Heritage Tour. This offers an opportunity to escape the frenzy of Kowloon and Central for unspoilt countryside, new towns and old villages, and see the relics of a far older China, including Tai Fu Tai Mansion, ancestral halls and walled villages. For details, enquire at HKTB offices or check www.discoverhongkong.com.

preserved traditional Chinese mansion in Hong Kong.

Man Mo Temple, Tai Po

Fu Shin Street, Tai Po; daily 9am–5pm; free, donations welcome; MTR: East line to Tai Wo

The Man Mo Temple in Tai Po was built about a century ago, and dedicated to the gods Man (literature) and Mo (martial arts). Built to mark the foundation of Tai Po New Market, this market-town temple was constructed as a walled compound to emphasise seclusion.

Tang Chung Ling Ancestral Hall

Lo Wai, near Fanling; Wed–Mon 9am–1pm, 2–5pm; free; MTR: East line to Fanling

Built in 1525, this hall dedicated to the ancestors of the local Tang clan was beautifully restored in 1922, and is still used for ceremonies. It boats exquisitely carved and colourful decorations.

Tsang Tai Uk

Near Sha Tin; MTR: East line to Sha Tin

Near the approach road to the Lion Rock tunnel, which carries the main road north

from Kowloon, this is an outstanding example of a fortified village. The name means 'Tsang's big house'; built in 1848, it is a large, rectangular grey brick compound with high thick walls and tall corner towers.

Temple of 10,000 Buddhas Monastery

Sha Tin; tel: 2691 1067; daily 9am–5pm; free, donations welcome; MTR: East line to Sha Tin (exit B)

There is a steep climb up to this monastery – dating only from the 1950s – but pilgrims are rewarded by the sight of actually well over 12,000 Buddha statues, nearly all slightly different from the next, lining the walls and stairways. There is also a mellow vegetarian restaurant.

Outer Islands

Po Lin Monastery and Tian Tan Buddha

Ngong Ping, Lantau Island; tel: 2985 5248; daily, monastery 9am–6pm, Buddha 10am–6pm; free, donations welcome; MTR: Tung Chung,

then bus: 23, or ferry: Mui Wo, then bus: 2, or Ngong Ping 360 cable car

Superlatives come thick and fast for the Tian Tan Buddha, the world's tallest seated outdoor bronze Buddha. Weighing 250 tonnes and perched at 34m (110ft) high, the statue towers above the fascinating Po Lin Monastery, high on the slopes of Lantau Island.

The monastery was founded in 1906 as a religious retreat, and visitors can wander through its temple complexes and lovely gardens, often full of exuberant orchids. To get a further sense of the Po Lin experience, be sure to sample the delicious vegetarian food served in the monastery's giant, canteen-style restaurants (daily 11.30am–5pm; tickets from the office below the Buddha). Nearby close to the terminal of the Ngong Ping 360 cable car is Ngong Ping village with new but attractive Ming dynasty-style buildings, tea shops, cafés and theatres.

Below: ascending to the Buddha at Po Lin Monastery.

Transport

Hong Kong is one of the most easily navigable cities on earth. Apart from its clean, cheap and efficient Mass Transit Railway system (known as the MTR), it has ferry services, tramlines on Hong Kong Island, excellent airport connections, a huge fleet of minibuses and squadrons of larger, double-decked buses, and more taxis than you could shake a stick at. Wheels aside, the city is laced with overhead walkways to help get people off the busy streets, and boasts the world's longest mechanical stairway, the Central-Mid-Levels Escalator, to ease the pain of Hong Kong Island's steep slopes.

Getting There by Air

Hong Kong is a major regional air-traffic hub, handling over 54 million passengers. Over 100 airlines operate flights to about 160 locations worldwide, including some 40 destinations in mainland China. Five airlines make the non-stop journey from the UK every day: Air New Zealand, British Airways, Cathay Pacific, Virgin Atlantic and Hongkong Airlines from Gatwick. If you don't mind connecting on your way, other European, Middle East-

ern and Asian carriers often offer much lower airfares to compensate for the added time required.

As the home and hub of **Cathay Pacific** (www.cathaypacific.com), Hong Kong is also a primary gateway to China: the airline flies on to destinations in mainland China, sometimes via sister airline, **Dragonair** (www.dragonair.com). **Virgin** (www.virgin-atlantic.com) flies on from Hong Kong to Sydney, **Air New Zealand** (www.airnewzealand.co.uk) continues on to Auckland and **Hongkong Airlines** (www.hongkongairlines.com) offers club class-only flights.

DIRECT FLIGHTS
These airlines fly direct to Hong Kong from the UK:
Air New Zealand
www.airnewzealand.co.uk
One flight a day from Heathrow.
British Airways
www.ba.com
Three flights per day from Heathrow.
Cathay Pacific
www.cathaypacific.com

Consider 'offsetting' the CO_2 from your journey to and around Hong Kong through an organisation like **Climate Care** (www.jpmorganclimatecare.org). Their online calculator will tell you your carbon emissions for your trip and how much you should donate to the scheme.

Four flights per day from Heathrow.
Virgin Atlantic
www.virgin-atlantic.com
One flight every day from Heathrow.

INDIRECT FLIGHTS
Airlines below fly between the UK and Hong Kong with one stop en route, which may mean changing planes.
Air France
www.airfrance.co.uk
Emirates
www.emirates.com
Finnair
www.finnair.co.uk
Lufthansa
www.lufthansa.com
Malaysia Airlines
www.malaysiaairlines.com
Qatar Airways
www.qatarairways.com

Terminal 2 at Hong Kong International Airport opened in March 2007. Alongside the existing Terminal 1, it contains 130 shops and restaurants plus four entertainment zones, in the Sky Plaza. T2 is the centrepiece of a larger development, Sky City, aimed at making HKIA an integrated 'airport city'. Other projects under development include a golf course, more hotels and – already in operation – the AsiaWorld-Expo site, with a giant-sized arena and exhibition spaces.

Left: know your Chinese road markings.

British Airways Holidays
Tel: 0844-493 0756;
www.baholidays.com
BA offers packages as well as flight and hotel combinations.

Cresta Holidays
Tel: 0844-800 7020;
www.crestaholidays.co.uk
A range of Hong Kong packages.

CTS Horizons
Tel: 020-7836 4338;
www.ctshorizons.com
Varied tours and tailor-made itineraries across China and Hong Kong.

Emerald Global (E-Tours Online)
Tel: 020-7312 1708;
www.etours-online.com
Asian travel specialist operator and flight consolidator with extremely competitive and exclusive flight prices.

Hayes and Jarvis
Tel: 0870-200 4422;
www.hayesandjarvis.co.uk
Long-established company offering an ample range of Hong Kong and China tours.

Oriental Travel
Tel: 020-7632 4550;
www.china-tour.co.uk
China and Hong Kong specialists, for small-group tours and individual itineraries.

Singapore Airlines
www.singaporeair.com
Thai Airways
www.thaiairways.com

Getting There by Sea

Hong Kong is a starting-off or end-point to a great number of cruise itineraries, and its status as a global airline hub also makes it a natural springboard for Asian fly-cruise itineraries. Costa, Crystal, Cunard, Regent Seven Seas, Seabourn, Royal Caribbean International, Holland America, P&O, Silversea, Peter Deilmann and Swan Hellenic are among the cruise lines that use Hong Kong. Many itineraries use Hong Kong as a base before sailing on to beach and island destinations in the region.

Cruise ships dock at the **Ocean Terminal** at the southernmost tip of Kowloon, in Tsim Sha Tsui, right next to the Harbour City mall. Until the Kai Tak cruise terminal opens, larger ships such as the *Queen Mary 2* moor at Kwai Chung Container terminal and ferry passengers to the Central Ferry Piers.

Hong Kong-based **Star Cruises** (www.starcruises.com) is one of a handful of lines offering overnight cruises into international waters where gambling is legal.

Tour Operators

UK tour operators that feature Hong Kong include:

Audley Travel
Tel: 01993-838 200;
www.audleytravel.com
Adventure trips in the whole of China, with Hong Kong as a base.

Below: rickshaws are often a quick option.

Above: taxis are available if their light is on.

Thomas Cook Signature
Tel: 0870-443 4447;
www.tcsignature.com
Low-priced Hong Kong
packages.

Thomson Worldwide
Tel: 0871-664 1100;
www.thomsonworldwide.com
Packages and itineraries.

Travelmood
Tel: 0800-0111 945;
www.travelmood.com
Good for Hong Kong and Bali
combinations, and stop-offs
en route to Australia.

To and from the Airport

The impressive and highly
efficient Norman Foster-
designed Hong Kong International Airport (HKIA) is at
Chek Lap Kok, on the northern shore of Lantau Island
and about 34km (21 miles)
from Central, which, as its
name suggests, is the urban
heart of Hong Kong Island.
Immigration queues are dealt
with swiftly, and suitcases
are often circling the carousel
by the time you reach the
baggage hall.

The eight-level airport
building is full of shops and
restaurants, as well as ATMs
and the excellent **Hong Kong
Tourist Board (HKTB)** information desks; be sure to collect the free welcome bag,
with a map, vouchers and

plenty of useful information.
There is a short-term baggage storage facility on Level
3 of Terminal 2.

All transport to the city
leaves from the **Ground
Transportation Centre**,
which is well signposted from
the Arrivals Hall. Details of all
services can be found on the
airport website.
SEE ALSO ESSENTIALS, P.39

Airport Information
Tel: 2181 8888;
www.hkairport.com

AIRPORT EXPRESS
The Airport Express railway,
part of the MTR system (see
opposite), runs from the
Ground Transportation
Centre in the terminal building, and is the quickest and
easiest way to get into town.

Street Signs

All street signs are in English
and Chinese. Hong Kong street
maps usually have both
English- and Chinese-language
sections in the back, to make it
easier to find your destination.
Be aware that while at times
the English name of a street or
district is a transliteration of the
Chinese, at others the Chinese
name is totally different and
may have no visible relation to
the English one.

All trains run to and from the
AsiaWorld-Expo exhibition
site alongside the airport, as
well as from the airport itself.
Trains reach Central station
on Hong Kong Island in just
23 minutes, with stops at
Tsing Yi and Kowloon. Trains
run in both directions daily
from 5.50am–1.15am, at 12
minute-intervals. Single tickets to Kowloon and Central
cost HK$90–100, returns
HK$160–180; children aged
under 11 travel for half the
adult fare.

Free **shuttle buses** run
between Central and
Kowloon Airport Express stations and many nearby
hotels. Most airlines allow
departing passengers to
check in baggage at Airport
Express stations, rather than
at the airport.

BUSES
Airbus services, prefixed **A**,
run at regular intervals to
Hong Kong Island, Kowloon
and the New Territories, and
there are also slower and still
cheaper 'commuter' buses
(prefixed **E**).

A11 and A12 run through
Central and the busiest areas
on Hong Kong Island, A21
through the heart of
Kowloon. Airbus fares to the
main urban areas range

Octopus Cards and Tourist Transport Passes

Anyone using public transport more than a couple of times will find it better, and cheaper, to get a multi-journey card than buy tickets each time you travel. Octopus is a stored-value smart card, valid on all kinds of transport except taxis and some minibuses and ferries, which can be bought at MTR stations. You pay a deposit of HK$50 for the card, and then charge it up for however much you want to spend (minimum HK$150). You then swipe the card on special machines each time you board a train, bus, tram and so on, and the fare is deducted. Octopus fares are always lower than those for single tickets, and Octopus holders also get discounts at a growing number of shops in Hong Kong. For details, see www.octopus cards.com. Transport Passes are more limited, and specially designed for visitors. The MTR 1-Day Tourist Pass gives you a day's unlimited travel on the MTR for HK$55; the 3-Day Transport Pass gives you three days' travel on MTR and some bus routes, including one (HK$220) or two (HK$300) Airport Express trips.

between HK$33 and HK$48, E-route fares from around HK$14–24. When you exit the Arrivals Hall, turn right for Airbuses or ordinary E-route buses. Route details are posted at the Transportation Centre, and on the airport website.

There are also night buses from the airport (prefixed N, which mostly run 12.20–5am), and shuttle buses to Tung Chung station, on the main MTR network. Long-distance buses also run to Guangzhou and other destinations in mainland China.

FERRIES

There are direct ferries from HKIA to Pearl River Delta destinations run by Chu Ku Passenger Transport (www. cksp.com.hk), while Turbojet runs ferries to Macau (www.turbojet.com.hk).

TAXIS

Taxis are easy to find, at the rank outside the Ground Transportation Centre. Urban taxis are red; New Territories taxis are green; local Lantau taxis are blue. A taxi to Central on Hong Kong Island will cost around HK$340 or more, to Kowloon slightly less; all fares from the airport include HK$30 toll for the Lantau island road bridge. Luggage is charged at HK$5 a piece.

Getting around the City

Although the high-rise jungles of Hong Kong may look daunting to the visitor, this is actually an easy city to get around, thanks to a highly efficient and easy-to-use public transport system. Rush hours, though (Mon–Fri roughly 8–10am and 5–7pm), can prove unpleasant for the uninitiated. Travelling at this time of day may make you feel less than charitable towards the local population as necessity has dictated

that people push in without ceremony to get onto buses, trains and trams.

To make the most of the system, use an **Octopus** travel card or a **Transport Pass** *(see left)* rather than single tickets. Children aged under 11 travel half-fare on most transport in Hong Kong, and under-3s travel free.

MASS TRANSIT RAILWAY (MTR)

The fast, efficient, very clean and air-conditioned MTR network operates daily from around 6am to 12.30–1am. As well as the Airport Express, the MTR comprises 10 lines, with 84 stations, with their hub at Central station on Hong Kong Island: the Island line (**royal blue** line, on maps and station signs) along the top of Hong Kong Island; the Tsuen Wan (**red**) line, from Central up through Kowloon to Tsuen Wan; the Tung Chung (**orange**) line, which flanks the Airport line out to Lantau; the Kwun Tong (**green**) line, from Yau Ma Tei in Kowloon out to East Kowloon; the Tseung Kwan O (**purple**) line between North Point on the island and East Kowloon; and the special Disneyland Resort line (**pink**), connecting the orange line to the resort.

Below: MTR sign.

Above: the latest in commutertainment.

Since merging with the former Kowloon Canton Railway the MTR East Rail line (**pale blue**) runs from East TST to the mainland border at Lo Wu and its sideline, the Ma On Shan (**brown**) line to Wu Kai Sha; the West Rail line (**violet**) line from East TST to Tuen Mun; and the separate **Light Rail** (yellow) between and around Tuen Mun and Yuen Long.

Travelling by MTR is quick, but a bit more expensive than going by bus or ferry. Adult single fares range from about HK$4–26 (but, as with all public transport, fares are lower with an Octopus card or Transport Pass, *see p.121*).

MTR stations have several exits, identified by letters and numbers, so it is good to have an idea of which you want (there are maps by each exit).

New lines are already under construction on Hong Kong Island including the West Island line through to Kennedy Town. The proposed South Island Line (East) from Admiralty to Ocean Park and Aberdeen is scheduled to be completed by 2015.

MTR Information
Tel: 2881 8888;
www.mtr.com.hk

BUSES
Six companies provide bus services in Hong Kong, but **Citybus** and the associated **New World First** have the most within the city. Buses cover every part of the Territory, but are most useful for areas not on the MTR or rail lines, such as the south side of Hong Kong Island and parts of the New Territories. Many routes start from or run through one of three termini, at Exchange Square, Central and the Admiralty Centre on Hong Kong Island, and by the Star Ferry Pier in Kowloon. Some routes run all night, with a less frequent service.

Most city buses are British-style double-deckers. Final destinations are marked in English and Chinese on the front. Drivers rarely speak much English, but timetables and route maps are posted at bus stops. Fares range from HK$3.50 for short journeys in the city to HK$45 for longer

Below: Peak Tram.

Taxi Talk
Many taxi drivers can speak some English, and will know the main hotels and tourist spots, but exchanges can at times be challenging. Drivers will sometimes refuse a fare, usually if the journey will take them out of their way as they are about to finish work (rather than try to argue, it is probably better to walk off and find another taxi). Ask your hotel concierge to write your destinations down in Chinese. All cabs are equipped with a radio phone, and somebody should be available to translate.

Above: double-decker bus.

trips into the New Territories.

Note, though, that **drivers do not carry change**, so that if you do not have an Octopus Card or Transport Pass you must have the exact money.

Bus Information
Citybus; tel: 2873 0818;
www.nwstbus.com.hk

Discovery Bay Transportation Services
Tel: 2238 1188; www.hkri.com
Serves part of Lantau Island.

Kowloon Motor Bus (KMB)
Tel: 2745 4466;
www.kmb.com.hk
Most Kowloon routes.

Long Win Bus Company
Tel: 2261 2791;
www.kmb.com.hk
Services to the airport.

New Lantao Bus Company
Tel: 2984 9848;
www.newlantaobus.com
Serves all of Lantau Island.

New World First Bus
Tel: 2136 8888;
www.nwfb.com.hk
City routes and many to the New Territories.

TRAMS

Trams have been rattling an east–west path along the north side of Hong Kong Island since 1904, and the double-decked carriages still offer a picturesque ride as well as an extremely inexpensive means of getting across the city. Stops are frequent, and the flat fare for each journey is HK$2.30, or HK$1.20 for under-12s and over 65s (exact change required, or use Octopus or Transport Pass); you get on at the back and get off at the front, paying as you get off. Tram routes operate between 5.45am and 11pm.

The **Peak Tram** is actually a funicular railway, and has been running since 1888. It takes eight minutes to reach the top from the terminus on Garden Road, Central (near Hong Kong Park). Trams run every 15 minutes, between 7am and midnight daily. The fare is HK$28 one-way, HK$40 return (Octopus and Transport Passes valid).

Hong Kong Tramways
Tel: 2548 7102;
www.hktramways.com

Peak Tram
Tel: 2522 0922;
www.thepeak.com.hk

MINIBUSES/MAXICABS

These 16-seater cream-coloured buses (with a red stripe) run on fixed routes, but stop anywhere except on double yellow lines. Once full they will not stop until requested. Destinations are usually written in English at the front of the van. Call out clearly when you want the driver to stop (try *'lee do'* in Cantonese). Fares vary from HK$4–20. Drivers will give change for small notes only, and 'green' minibuses accept Octopus Cards.

TAXIS

Taxis are cheap, abundant and easy to hail on the street, although in rush hours you may need to join a queue at a rank or a hotel. Taxis in Hong Kong Island and Kowloon are red, and in theory can take you anywhere apart from non-airport destinations on Lantau. Sometimes you will come across taxis on Hong Kong Island which are so-called 'Kowloon taxis', and will only take passengers across to Kowloon. Green taxis run in the New Territories, blue ones on Lantau.

Minimum fare for red cabs is HK$18, and there are extra charges for luggage placed in the car boot, and tunnel and bridge tolls. Many, but not all, taxi drivers speak reasonable English; all fares are metered, and receipts given. By law all passengers must wear seat belts, and drivers will remind you if you do not buckle up. If possible, avoid taking taxis in rush hours, when journeys can take twice as long.

Below: getting around is aided by bilingual signage.

Above: the Star Ferry carries passengers across Victoria Harbour.

STAR FERRY

The traditional cross-harbour ferries are a Hong Kong institution, and a ride ranks as one of the best and cheapest sightseeing thrills. The 12-strong Star Ferry fleet of open-sided ferries still run between Central and Wan Chai on Hong Kong Island and Kowloon from 6.30am–11.30pm every day. Fares begin at just HK$1.70 (HK$2.20 on the upper deck) on the main Central to Tsim Sha Tsui route. Departures are every 6–12 minutes depending on the time of day, and the trip takes about eight minutes.

More modern New World Ferries also run across the harbour from North Point to Hung Hom. **Star Ferry Information** Tel: 2367 7065; www.starferry.com.hk

Out of Town

Urban Hong Kong makes up only part of the Territory. Beyond the 24-hour bustle and intense cityscape extend dramatic scenery, traditional villages, serene monasteries, beaches and hundreds of smaller, tranquil islands, all still easily accessible, thanks to the local transport system. The Pearl River also connects Hong Kong with the former Portuguese colony of Macau, and China's Guangdong province. Day trips to both are easy to do. For bus information, *see p.122*.

FERRIES TO OUTLYING ISLANDS

Ferries to Lamma, Lantau (including a 24-hour service to Discovery Bay), Cheung Chau and other islands leave from the **Central Ferry Piers**, just north of the Airport Express station in Central on Hong Kong Island.

Two types operate on most routes: **standard** ferries and the slightly more expensive **fast** ferries. New World First Ferry has the most routes.

Fares vary greatly but start from HK$12.60, and can be double at weekends and holidays. Octopus Cards *(see p.121)* can be used on most ferries; otherwise, take correct change for the ticket turnstile; change booths are only open at peak times. If visiting Lamma, be aware that there are two channels at Pier 4, one for ferries to Yung Shue Wan (north), the other for Sok Kwu Wan (east).

FERRY INFORMATION
Discovery Bay
Transportation Services
Tel: 2238 1188; www.hkri.com
Ferries to the south side of Lantau.
Hong Kong
Kowloon Ferry
Tel: 2815 6063;
www.hkkf.com.hk
Ferries to Lamma.
New World First Ferry
Tel: 2131 8181;
www.nwff.com.hk
Ferries for most of the islands.

TO MACAU

There are very frequent ferry sailings every day between Hong Kong and Macau, 65km (40 miles) to the west, from two departure points: the **Macau Ferry Terminal** in in the **Shun Tak Centre** Sheung Wan, near the Central

Top Views

Topping out the list of Hong Kong's excellent network of transport ferrying commuters and residents about the city, the city also has some extra transport options that ensure you get the very best views of the city. **Citybus** runs two hop-on hop-off bus tours on its distinctive pink open-top Rickshaw Sightseeing Bus from the Star Ferry Central Pier 7 (www.rickshawbus.com). Full-day fares are HK$50 for adults, HK$25 for children. The Heritage Route runs around historic sights in Central and Western District (daily 10am–7.30pm) the Metropolis Route takes in the Peak Tram terminal, Wan Chai and Causeway Bay (10.15am–9.45pm). From Tung Chung MTR station on Lantau Island the **Ngong Ping 360 cable car** (www.np360.com.hk; Mon–Fri 10am–6pm, Sat–Sun 9am–6.30pm), takes the strain out of a trip to the Big Buddha with truly breathtaking views of North Lantau and the South China Sea. Some cabins feature glass floors to make the 25-minute journey even more thrilling. From here you will get a spectacular birds-eye view. Wheelchair bound passengers can easily go on board. Children under 11 must be accompanied by an adult.
The cable cars have regular service days and weather can be an issue, so it is best to check it is operating before setting out for Lantau to avoid disappointment.

Ferry Piers, and the **China Ferry Terminal** in Tsim Sha Tsui, Kowloon. Turbojet also runs direct ferry transfers from Hong Kong Airport.

It is wise to buy return tickets on Macau ferries in advance, especially at weekends or holidays, as seats can sell out. Fares vary between ferry services, and according to the class of ticket, which day and at what time you travel. For up-to-date information, check with individual companies, or the Macau Government Tourist Office, tel: 2838 8680, www.macautourism.gov.mo.

Turbojet offers the most frequent service, from Macau Ferry Terminal. Ferries leave every 15 minutes 7am–1am, and once an hour during the night, and the crossing takes 55–65 minutes. Tickets generally cost HK$151–185, 'ordinary class', one-way.

CotaiJet (www.cotaijet.com.mo) runs ferries from Macau Ferry Terminal to Taipa, close to the Cotai casinos every half hour 6.30am–12am. Tickets cost HK$151–185, 'ordinary class', one-way.

New World First Ferry runs high-speed catamarans from the China Ferry Terminal. They leave every half-hour, 7am–midnight, and journey time is 65–75 minutes. Ordinary-class single fares are HK$151–185.

Macau Ferry Information

New World First Ferry; tel: 2131 8181; www.nwff.com.hk
Turbojet; tel: 2859 3333; www.turbojet.com.hk

TO CHINA

Guangzhou (formerly Canton), and the rural landscapes around Shenzhen lie only 45 minutes from Hong Kong by train or bus. Most travellers will need to obtain a visa to enter mainland China (see p.39).

Train tickets can be bought online at CTS (China Travel Service) branches or at Hong Kong travel agents. Trains arrive at Guangzhou East station, a taxi ride from the city centre.

Buses are a slower, even cheaper, alternative. CTS also has an extensive bus network, with daily departures from Hong Kong.

Ferries also ply between Hong Kong and several Guangdong cities including Zhuhai, Shekou and Fuyong (for Shenzhen Airport) from China Ferry Terminal in Tsim Sha Tsui, Shun Tak Centre, Sheung Wan and Hong Kong Airport; passengers on this route clear immigration into China, not Hong Kong. **Turbojet** has the most modern services.

China Transport Information

MTR; tel: 2881 8888
China Travel Service (CTS); tel: 2851 1700; www.ctshk.com
Turbojet; tel: 2859 3333; www.turbojet.com.hk

Below: all aboard, no frowns please.

Walks and Views

If there is one thing Hong Kong is not short of, it is stupendous views. Whether you are up at the Peak, sitting on the upper deck of a tram or exploring the outlying islands, you are almost guaranteed a good view of a spectacular city set in a fantastic natural environment. Take the time to explore on foot and you will be justly rewarded. In parts of the New Territories and outlying islands it is possible to take long walks in dramatic mountain scenery, enjoy superb natural views and see barely a soul for hours and hours. It is difficult to believe that the hectic Central is only minutes away.

The Peak

Start/End: Peak Tower, Lugard Road; www.thepeak.com.hk; daily 7am–midnight; tram to Peak Tower, bus 15

One of the main reasons people ascend the Peak – as well as the tram ride to get there – is to marvel at some of the world's finest vistas. On one of Hong Kong's (increasingly rare) clear days there should be a view all the way to mainland China. Many find the night-time views – a vast glittering swathe of electric light – even more spectacular. The **Peak Tower**, next to the top of the tramway, was renovated in 2006, adding new shops, restaurants, and significantly more windows to make the most of the views. The viewing platform has

An ample supply of information is available to visitors aiming to explore Hong Kong's hiking possibilities. HKTB Tourist Offices provide advice, free maps and a series of Hong Kong Walks and Heritage Trails leaflets. Anyone with a bit more time can also find a choice of good walking guides in bookshops, of which the Heritage, *Leisurely* or *Serious Hiker's Guides to Hong Kong*, by Pete Spurrier, are among the best. The shop at the GPO in Central is a good resource for maps.

been raised 30m (100ft) to the top of the so-called 'wok' for a 360-degree panorama.

WALKS FROM THE PEAK
Peak Circle Walk

Start: Peak Tower; tram to Peak Tower, bus 15

End: Garden Road Terminus; bus 12S, 15C; map 137 D2

There are a variety of superb walks from the Peak. The Peak Circle Walk follows Lugard and Harlech roads from the Peak Tower, affording magnificent views across the harbour to Kowloon in the north; to Cheung Chau and Lantau to the west; and over the great mass of junks and sampans at Aberdeen to the south, with Lamma Island's telltale chimney stacks beyond. This gentle 3km (2-mile) walk, well signposted and shaded from the sun, is about a 45 minute-round-trip from the Tower.

The area around the Peak Tower is in fact **Victoria Gap**, whereas the summit of **Victoria Peak** itself (552m/1,800ft)

Left: view off the south side of Hong Kong Island.

Left. Dragon's Back trail is a walk for the brave.

Heritage Hunters

As part of the city's newfound interest in its heritage, a number of trails have been designed for locals and visitors, taking in notable buildings or sites of historic events. On Hong Kong Island there are routes covering, Sheung Wan, Central, Wan Chai, Tai Tam and Western District. Route maps and information are available online at the Antiquities and Monuments Office (www.amo.gov.hk) and from the Hong Kong Heritage Discovery Centre in Kowloon Park. With these route maps, venture to the New Territories where the Ping Shan and Lung Yuk Tau Heritage trails are easy to find and reveal even more of Hong Kong' contrasts.

Lung Yuk Tau Heritage Trail

Start: Fanling MTR station, then 54K minibus
Finish: Siu Hang Tsuen
Take in a mix of centuries old buildings and walled villages. Start at Shung Him Tong, a village founded in 1901 by Hakka Lutherans fleeing persecution across the border. The trail ends at the considerably older Tang Chung Ling Ancestral Hall (Wed–Mon 9am–1pm, 2–5pm; free). Originally built in 1570, the hall remains a focal point of the Tang clan.

looms up just to the west. Follow the Peak Circle Walk until you reach the **Governor's Walk**, which winds up to the attractive **Victoria Peak Garden**. The summit itself is out of bounds.

It is also possible to walk back down to the city from the Peak, and enjoy some of the best views and footpaths around its wooded slopes. The **Central Green Trail** – marked by 14 bilingual signboards highlighting points of interest – meanders from Barker Road, a little below the Peak Tower, down across May Road and then via paths named Clovelly, Brewin and Tramway back to the Garden Road tram station.

Hong Kong Trail

Start: Peak Tower; tram to Peak Tower, bus 15
End: Peel Rise; bus 7, 37B, 38, 42, 70, 71, 90B, 91, 94, 107, 970, 973
A popular longer walk continues westwards from the Peak Circle. Walk through **Pok Fu Lam Country Park**. This path joins up with the **Hong Kong Trail**, which curves around Pok Fu Lam before heading

east along the ridges above Aberdeen to wind right across Hong Kong Island all the way to Tai Tam and Shek O, a full distance of 50km (30 miles). Nature-lovers can wander through forests of bamboo and fern, stunted Chinese pines, hibiscus and a jumble of vines, with a good amount of shade. If you do not want to take on the whole trail, there are various points where you can cut off and find buses back to the city.

Dragon's Back

Start: MTR: Shau Kei Wan exit A3 bus 9 towards Shek O.
End: Shek O

Below: an unexpected guest.

Above: a trail through Tai Tam Country Park.

One of the most straightforward trails. Get off the bus at the ninth stop – To Tei Wan, where you'll see a bus shelter, steps, a detailed map and Shek O Country Park signs. Once you've reached the top of the 'back' it's an easy walk along the open ridge overlooking Eastern approaches towards the Clearwater Bay peninsula and Tung Lung Island before dropping down into Shek O where you can feast at open-air restaurants.

Central and Western Districts

MTR: Sheung Wan; map p.136 B4

The districts of Sheung Wan and around Hollywood Road are among the most characterful – and oldest – parts of Hong Kong city, and so some of the most popular areas for exploratory urban walks. You will be so mesmerised by the street life, you will barely notice your legs moving.

October through to June are the best months for walking in Hong Kong when the temperature drops below 30 degrees and humidity lessens. Make sure you always have enough water and carry a mobile phone.

Sheung Wan

Start: Western Market, Connaught and Morrison; Sheung Wan MTR; map 136 B4
End: Mid-Levels Escalator; Central MTR; map 136 C3

Begin at **Western Market** *(see p.103)*, a large red-brick Edwardian building a short way west of Sheung Wan MTR. Turn left (away from the harbour) into **Morrison Street**, and immediately right into **Wing Lok Street**, where you will find numerous speciality shops selling ginseng and the so-called, much-prized 'bird's nest' used in soup, gathered from the sides of caves. At the end of this street turn left into **Des Voeux Road West** – home to little shops displaying huge varieties of exotic dried seafood – and then left again into **Ko Shing Street**, the wholesale centre for Hong Kong's thriving herbal medicine trade. It is easy to wander for hours, trying to figure exactly what the wares on show – rare plants, dried animal organs – could be.

Hollywood Road

To compare Sheung Wan with its less pungent but still atmospheric neighbour, walk back to Des Voeux Road West, and turn right into Bon-

ham Strand West (parallel to Wing Lok) and then right again into Possession Street. From here the road slopes upwards to meet Hollywood Road, famous for its curios and antiques shops. Head left, and when you have done browsing continue on to the famous Man Mo Temple, with maybe a detour left into Upper Lascar Row (Cat Street Bazaar) for more browsing among traditional Chinese carvings, antiques and oddities, rejoining Hollywood Road at Ladder Street.

Inside Man Mo *(see p.114)* the air is thick with aromatic smoke from the incense coils dangling from its roof. Carry on along Hollywood Road to reach the **Mid-Levels Escalator**. From here you can explore SoHo, or wind down into Central.

Tai Tam Country Park

Start: Tai Tam Country Park; bus 6, 66
End: Tai Tam Road; bus 14, 314

The Tai Tam reservoirs that lie in the southeast of Hong Kong Island offer an oasis of calm for walkers. This is a relatively easy downhill walk, which passes many good picnic stops, beautiful surroundings and the calm, still waters of the reservoirs.

Set off from **Park View**, above Causeway Bay on the **Wong Nai Chung Gap** road to Repulse Bay and Stanley (if you take the 6 or 66 bus from Exchange Square, get off at the Wong Nai Chung Reservoir). Follow the road that turns east off the main road downhill past **Hong Kong Parkview**, down past a picnic area, cross the dam and turn right. The stream leaving the first reservoir is hidden in a wooded ravine.

Cross the bridge below the **Tai Tam Intermediate** reservoir, and pause at the pavilion on the left for a view over the bigger **Tai Tam Tuk** reservoir. Keep to the road beside this reservoir and walk its length before crossing over a picturesque bridge. Within 10 minutes or so you will arrive at **Tai Tam Road**. From here you can catch a bus (14, 314) back to the city.

Lamma

Start: Central Pier 4 Yung Shue Wan Terminal; ferry to Lamma
End: Sok Kwu Kwan; ferry to Central (Hong Kong Kowloon Ferry; tel: 2815 6063, www.hkkf.com.hk)
The gently rolling, north-to-south walk between Lamma's ferry piers takes a couple of hours and will give you a flavour of both sides of the island, as well as rewarding you with some of its most beautiful views. Take the ferry to **Yung Shue Wan** on the north side, and, after strolling through the village (10 minutes), follow signs indicating a left turn to **Hung Shing Ye**. Keep the three chimneys of Lamma Power Station looming ever-present on your right.

Hung Shing Ye Beach is

relatively clean, with changing rooms, a small hotel with a café, and Herboland organic farm. At the far end of the beach the narrow concrete path starts to climb more steeply towards a hill with an observation pavilion. This is a good halfway point if you want to head back.

The reward for carrying on to **Sok Kwu Wan** on the east side of Lamma becomes immediately apparent as the path winds around the mountain, opening up fabulous sea views to your right. The walking is not strenuous, and before long the path begins to descend into **Lo So Shing**, a sleepy hamlet of traditional village houses.

From the village, either follow the signs to the pretty (and relatively secluded) **Lo So Shing Beach** or continue directly to **Sok Kwu Wan** (Picnic Bay). Stop for lunch or dinner at one of the string of waterfront seafood restaurants, before catching a ferry back to Central (check times before eating).

Although Lamma is famous for not having any conventional motor vehicles, watch out for small trucks called 'vil-lage vehicles', which are sometimes driven along footpaths pretty aggressively.

Lantau

Start: Po Lin Monastery; ferry to Lantau from outlying islands
End: Lantau Peak; ferry to Central from outlying islands (Ferries Ferry Terminal, *see p.124*, or MTR: Tung Ching, then local buses)
The centre of Lantau Island is dominated by lofty mountains, the most notable of these being Lantau Peak and Sunset Peak. These peaks are criss-crossed with winding pathways and trails, linking several Buddhist monasteries. From the **Po Lin Monastery**, follow the sign to the **Tea Garden**, and at the entrance follow the hiking trail for about 15 minutes. If you have time, pause at the **Wisdom Path** on your left. Otherwise, look for the entrance gate leading to **Lantau Peak**. Much of the route wanders through substantial natural woodland, with hillside streams crossing the trail. The peak is on your right, and this trail winds around its northern slopes.
SEE ALSO TEMPLES AND HISTORIC SITES, P.117

Right: climbing plant.

Atlas

The following streetplan of Hong Kong makes it easy to find the attractions listed in our A–Z section. A selective index to streets and sights will help you find other locations throughout the city

Map Legend

▨	Notable building	ⓘ	Tourist information
▨	Market / Mall / Store	★	Sight of interest
▨	Transport hub	Ⓜ	Metro (MTR) station
▨	Hotel	🚌	Bus station
▢	Urban area	☾	Mosque
▢	Pedestrian area	✡	Synagogue
⬚	Aerial walkway	✝	Cathedral / church
▢	Park	✉	Post office
▢	Non-urban area	♒	Radio tower
▢	Tunnel	Ⓜ	Museum
✝✝	Cemetery	🎭	Theatre
		⚊	Statue / monument

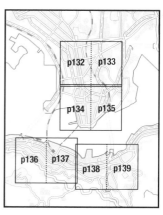

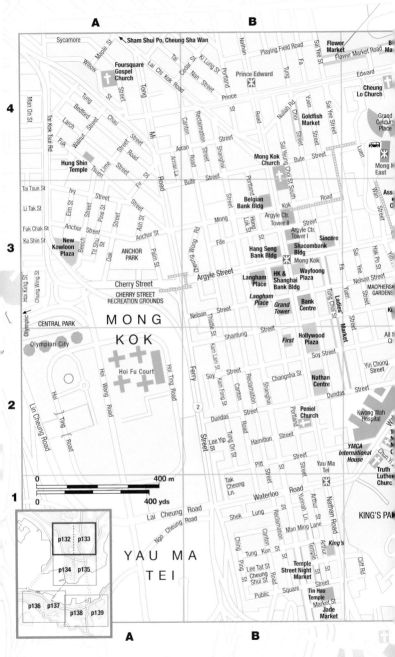

A · B

Sycamore
Maple St
Sham Shui Po, Cheung Sha Wan
Ki Lung St
Playing Field Road
Sai Yee St
Flower Market
Flower Market Road
B Ma

Willow
Tai
Cedar St
Nan Street
Portland
Nathan
Fa
Tung
Edward

Foursquare Gospel Church
Lai Chi Kok Road
Tong
Street
Prince Edward
Prince St
Yuen St
Choi St
Cheung Lo Church

Tung
Bedford Street
Chau Street
Mi
Canton
Reclamation
Street
Road
Sai Yeung Choi Street
Bute Street
Goldfish Market
Grand Century Place

Man On St
Tai Kok Tsui Rd
Larch
Walnut Street
Street
Arran Road
Shanghai
Mong Kok Church
Sai Yeung Choi St South
Mong East

Fuk
Tsuen Lime Street
Fir
Arran La
Street
Bute
Kok Road
Ass C

Hung Shin Temple
Street
Bute Street
Portland
Belgian Bank Bldg
Street

Tai Tsun St
Ivy Street
Elm St
Pine St
Asp St
Street
Mong
Hong Lok St
Argyle Ctr. Tower II
Street
Wan

Li Tak St
Anchor Street
Kok Rd
Fife
Argyle Ctr. Tower I
Sincere
Sai

Fuk Chak St
Beech
Tit Shu St
Oak
Anchor St
Mong Kwong Rd
Hang Seng Bank Bldg
Shacombank Bldg
Mong Kok
Hak Po St
Yiu

Ka Shin St
New Kowloon Plaza
ANCHOR PARK
Palm St
Wayfoong Plaza
Fa
Nelson Street
MACPHERS GARDENS

Cheung Wing St
Hoi King St
Cherry Street
CHERRY STREET RECREATION GROUNDS
Argyle Street
Langham Place
HK & Shanghai Bank Bldg
Tung Choi St
Ladies' Street Market
Ku

Olympic
Nelson Street
Langham Place
Grand Tower
Bank Centre
All C

CENTRAL PARK
M O N G
Thistle St
Shantung
Street
First
Hollywood Plaza

Olympian City
K O K
Kam Lam St
Soy Street
Yin Chong Street

Hoi Wang Road
Hoi Fu Court
Hoi Ting Road
Ferry
Soy Street
Kam Fong St
Changsha St
Reclamation
Shanghai
Nathan Centre
Dundas
Street

Lin Cheung Road
Hoi
Ting
Road
2
Dundas Street
Canton
Portland
Peniel Church
Kwong Wah Hospital
W N C

Street
Lee Yip St
Tung On St
Hamilton
Street
YMCA International House
Chiu V

Pitt St
Street
Yau Ma Tei
Truth Luther Churc

0   400 m
0   400 yds

Tak Cheong Ln.
Waterloo
Road
Yunnam
Lung
Arthur
Nathan Road
KING'S PA

Lai Cheung Road
Ngo Cheung Road
Shek
Lung
Man Ming Lane
Arthur St

YAU MA TEI
Ching
Tung Kun St
Canton
Reclamation
Temple
King's

Ping
Lee Tat St
Cheung Shui St
Road
Temple Street Night Market
St
Cliff Rd

Public
Square
Tin Hau Temple
Market St
Jade Market

p132 | p133
p134 | p135
p136 | p137 | p138 | p139

A · B

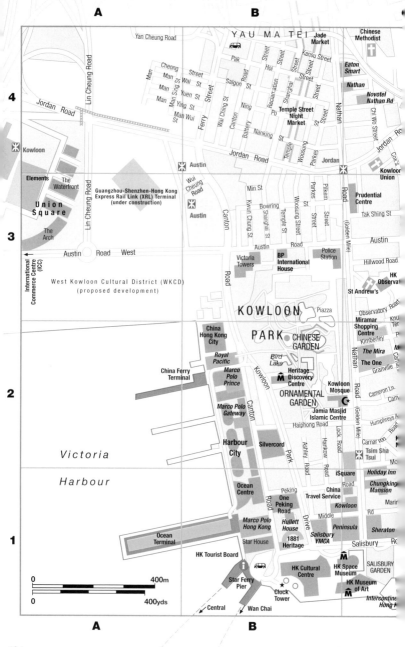

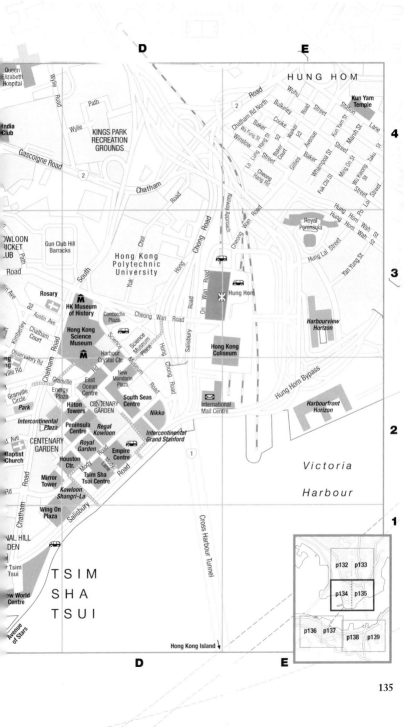

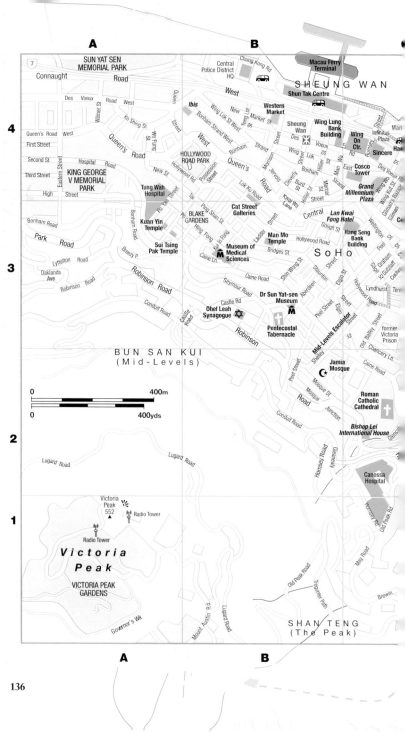

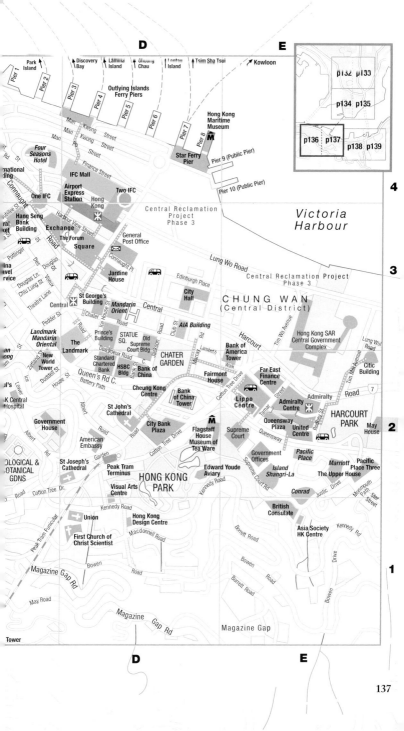

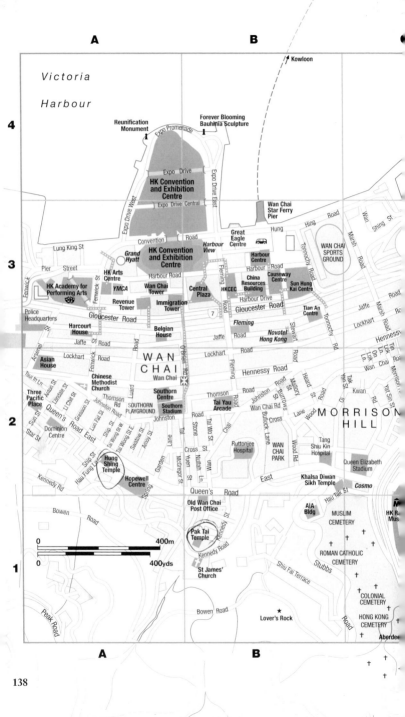

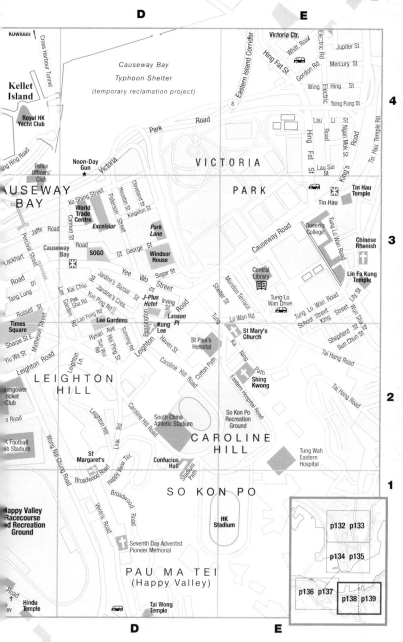

Selective Index for Street Atlas

Index

Insight Smart Guide: Hong Kong
Text by: **Ryan Levitt, Teresa Machan**
Updated by: **Ruth Williams**
Commissioned by: **Rebecca Lovell**
Edited by: **Paula Soper**
Photography by: **Alex Havret/apa,**
except Corbis 41B; Disneyland Hong Kong 28; Getty 48BL&BR, 48/49T, 49C, 51BC&B, 69B; Glyn Genin/APA 34; Government Information Services 51T; Harbour Plaza Hotel 55; Intercontinental Hong Kong 56; Island Shangri-La 53BL&BR; iStockphoto 5, 22, 30, 37, 65, 73,88, 89, 92; Gerhard Joren 51TC; Leonardo 52–53; Mary Evans Picture Library 50CB; Manfred Morgenstern 50TC& B, 51TC
Designer: **Richard Cooke**
Maps: **James Macdonald and Neal Jordan-Caws**
Series Editor: **Carine Tracanelli**

Third Edition 2012
© 2012 Apa Publications UK Ltd
Printed by CTPS-China

Worldwide distribution enquiries:
APA Publications GmbH & Co Verlag KG (Singapore branch); 7030 Ang Mo Kio Ave 5, 08-65 Northstar @ AMK, Singapore 569880; email: apasin@signet.com.sg
Distributed in the UK and Ireland by:
Dorling Kindersley Ltd (a Penguin Company); 80 Strand, London, WC2R 0RL, UK; email: customerservice@uk.dk.com
Distributed in Australia by:
Universal Publishers; PO Box 307, St. Leonards, NSW 1590; email: sales@universalpublishers.com.au
Distributed in New Zealand by:
Brown Knows Publications; 11 Artesia Close, Shamrock Park, Auckland, New Zealand 2016; email: sales@brownknows.co.nz